Down Our Road

Nature Musings from the Northwoods

by
Jean E. Dohms

Copyright 1995 by Boulder Knob Books
P.O. Box 210
Crystal Falls, MI 49920

Illustrations by
Beth Sjostrom

Cover photograph by
Paula Sykora

Library of Congress Card No. 95-094245
ISBN #0-9645665-0-8

Printed in Michigan, U.S.A.

To the attentive eye, each moment of the year has its own beauty, and in the same field it beholds every hour a picture which was never seen before and which shall never be seen again.

Ralph Waldo Emerson in *Nature.*

Table of Contents

Preface

I was born lucky. Not everyone is fortunate to have a father who loved the outdoors, and a mother who loved books. These factors, plus a heritage of pioneer ancestors, probably contributed to my curiosity about the natural world.

Every summer from the time I was six until I was eighteen, I went to Camp Fire Girls' camps. These camps were crude by today's standards, but there I slept under the stars, went canoeing at dawn, learned to build a fire, and most important, to appreciate the diversity of Nature's offerings.

My good fortune didn't end there. For fifty two years I have been married to a man who has encouraged me in all my endeavors. My Old Sea Dog, ex-sea captain, stood behind me when I spent six years going to college at night for my undergraduate degree. He met my train and had dinner and a cold drink waiting for me the three years that I spent getting my master's degree in library science at fifty-five. Best of all, after we both retired, he followed me to my inherited home in the northwoods in Michigan's Upper Peninsula.

Here, in this Superior land, we have made our home at the end of the road, above a beautiful lake, surrounded by deep woods, an old potato farm, and magnificent conifers.

When a newspaper editor called me and asked me if I would like to do a column for the local paper, at first I said no. But then, I thought, "You call yourself a writer; prove it."

My column began in the summer, and so do these chapters. Up here in the northwoods, we dream of our all too short summers. So this book will begin and end with the zenith of the life cycle of the plants and animals, the continuation of the species, and our joy at being a spectator to the wonders of God's world.

Summer

Down Our Road

In the summer, after the dishes are done, my husband and I go for our evening constitutional. Every walk is an adventure. We never know what animals we'll see or hear, or what plants will be in bloom.

It is a half mile to the mail boxes on the county road, and this half mile takes us past stone walled fields, an ancient apple orchard, an old wood with tall sugar maple and stately hemlock, and another wood of second growth aspen.

Usually the noises we hear on our walks are peaceful — the drumming of the downy woodpecker, the caw of the crow, or the snort of the mother deer warning her fawn of our presence.

But last week an ungodly repetitive noise stopped us in our tracks. The racket was coming from the woods at the far end of the field. At first we thought it was an animal caught in a trap. It was a combination of a yelp, screech, and a howl. Something or someone was being tortured. It went on and on. It didn't quite sound like a dog. It wasn't like any owl I had ever heard. The clamor continued, but the "thing" making all that hullabaloo was finally moving through the trees.

We continued on our walk. In about ten minutes all was quiet. We breathed a sigh of relief.

Could it have been the bobcat that we had seen the week before? Friends have suggested that this is a possibility. We'll probably never know, but it was a noise I'd rather not hear again.

On this walk, the woods were quiet. It had rained heavily during the afternoon and as we passed the fields we caught that wonderful scent of milk weed blossoms, and red clover.

I stopped for wild raspberries growing in the ditch. Their flavor was winey and very sweet. Not too many, just a tantalizing taste. I had to run and catch up with my Old Sea Dog who was reminding me that the object of this walk, was exercise!

Here and there were spots of deep blue in the grass where heal-all grows. It is also called self-heal, carpenter's herb, hook-heal, and sicklewort. If only all the small tubular, two lipped, hooded flowers bloomed at the same time, it would make a wonderful addition to the flower garden. The latin name is Prunella vulgaris, and it is a member of the mint family. As with all mints, it has a square stem and opposite leaves. The flower head is almost square. It doesn't have the mint smell.

Prunella is an herb, known to the early settlers, but also used by the Indians, who called it wuskons. The Indians used it combined with catnip for diseases of the digestive system. In England it was considered a certain cure for quinsy throat. As its many names imply, the herb was applied by rustic laborers to wounds. The French had an old proverb, "No one wants a surgeon who keeps Prunella."

Instead of returning by the road, we cut across the field behind the stone wall. The hill rises more slowly to the barn at the back of our property. It's easier on our old legs.

The big barn is the only remaining structure of the turn of the century Finnish potato farm. The homestead is now a pile of fallen beams, old plaster, and roofing. The weeds are knee high and mixed with blackberry and wild rose brambles.

Everywhere are reminders of the past. The thousands of rocks that border the field were hand picked, and dragged by horse drawn stone-boats to make the walls. Rocks too big, were buried deeper, manually!

Once loving hands planted lilacs, the old fashioned pale lavender ones. They still bloom, and this year they were more beautiful than I can remember — huge clumps of sweet scented blossoms.

There had been a flower garden on the south side of the house. When we bought the property all that remained were a few old fashioned yellow iris and a clump of pink peonies.

Last year the old apple tree, near the house, still had a few lovely blossoms and in the fall some misshapen fruit. This summer it is only a skeleton.

There is still an old asparagus bed. The stems of the plants are about an inch and a half around, but tender. An old rhubarb patch remains with five pie plants.

The orchard was away from the house and the potato field. Years ago there had been several species, early transparents, crab apples, and one which tasted much like a mackintosh. In the last thirty five years these trees have died off one by one, until there are only three bearing trees left, just enough for the deer to enjoy in the fall. Underneath the rubble of the house we can still see the remnants of the fruit cellar where broken glass Ball jars litter the earthen floor. These are the same kind that I remember my mother using in the 1920s, the kind with the rubber rings and screw-on tops. Canning was a necessity for this large family.

Close to the house the family had dug a large root cellar into the side of a hill. It was probably used to store their potatoes. Last year, a vixen found it to be an ideal place to raise her family.

We got to know the son of these hard-working people. Leonard loved to come out and visit my mother and father and bring his son. He loved that land, and had been heartbroken when his family sold the farm while he was overseas during World War II.

We liked to walk with Leonard while he told us about the log buildings. "This was our horse barn. We couldn't keep them in the same barn as the cows. They would get sick from too much moisture."

"Here I had my tool shed, and that was the sauna."

One time Leonard brought his brother, Everett, from California and his brother's son. The old men wandered slowly around the farm, reminiscing. "That was where mother kept the chickens. Remember how we dug the well, that was something."

The O.S.D. asked the question. "Did you dig it by hand?"

"Yes, we three boys took turns digging and shoring up the sides, while the others took out the soil. We went down 125 feet and hit hard pan," Everett remembered.

"We built an A-frame and suspended a drill point. We dropped it time after time. Finally we broke through, but still no water," Leonard continued.

"It was early spring and there was a pond of melting snow. We took a fire hose and filled it, and lowered it down to Emil below. That did the trick, but boy did Emil have to scramble to get out of there. He sure was mad. We had a hard time capping it too, but we had good water to pump."

Those were hard times.

Last month I had braved the tall grass with the hidden wood ticks to check-out Mrs. Pesonens heritage. I came back with six stalks of asparagus, a handful of rhubarb, a bouquet of lilacs, and THREE TICKS.

That night we had fresh asparagus with our ham, and vanilla ice cream with rhubarb sauce at a table with a vase of beautiful lilacs, and we celebrated those wonderful hard-working people.

Raspberry Picking

Two beautiful, sunny August days in a row, and not too hot. This was the morning to go raspberry picking. The man of my house loves seeded wild raspberry jam on his morning toast. We had only half a jar left.

I had thought that the berries weren't going to be good this year, but after the heavy rain, and now the sun, they were lush.

I headed for our best berry patch under the shade of six old gnarled apple trees, at the edge of our field.

The morning stillness was broken only by the distant drone of a motorboat. The boat must have gotten too close to a loon, for I could hear his wailing protest. It's always good to know that these endangered birds are still with us.

I slowly began to fill my plastic bucket with the hidden berries. I won't be needing to put on my exercise tape with all the stretching, reaching and bending it takes to find these elusive rubies.

I was proud of myself, I only ate three. The best, in my mind, are those deep red ones that are about to fall. Sweet, but tart.

Two years ago, when I was picking in this patch, I heard a noise on the other side of the bushes. It was a large skunk enjoying the fruit. I decided he had priority that day.

In many places the bracken is as tall as the raspberries. A huge sumac bush is loaded with its red fruit. A sour lemony, drink can be made of these, but today it's raspberries I'm after.

A chipmunk runs across the stone wall. He stops and scolds me. He is probably annoyed that I'm picking "his" berries. A small flock of chickadees land in the apple tree. One gives his sweet phee-bee whistle. The others chatter together and chickadee-dee-dee at me and each other. I wish they knew that my husband and I are trying to make them the State Bird of Michigan instead of the robin.

In between the raspberry bushes the agrimony grows everywhere. Fortunately, only a few of the burs are ripe. Before their sticky seeds are formed, the small yellow flowers are very attractive. Each year I promise myself that I'll try using them to dye a tee shirt. All my herb books say that it produces a beautiful yellow color, especially in the fall. I've even gone as far as buying alum and cream of tartar for mordant, but each day flies by. Oh, well, I don't wear tee shirts anymore.

I'm a collector of books, especially reference books. I must have at least twenty herbals. I looked up agrimony again. Nicolas Culpeper (1616-1654), the English astrologer/apothecary, describes Agrimony (Agrimonia gryposepala) in his *Complete Herbal:*

"This hath divers long leaves, some greater, some smaller, set upon a stalk, all of them, dented about the edges, green above and greyish underneath, and a little hairy withal; among which ariseth up usually but one strong, round hairy, brown stalk two or three feet high with smaller leaves set here and there upon it. At the top hereof grow many small yellow flowers, one above another, in long spikes, after which come round heads of seed, hanging downwards, which will cleave to and stick upon garments, or any thing that shall rub against them."

Besides being an apothecary, Culpeper was a Puritan. He conducted a campaign against the monopoly of the College of Physicians. In 1649 he published an English translation of the college's *Pharmacopoeia*, so that the common people could use the cures God provided. Of course, this brought down the wrath of the physicians, but his herbals went on to become a best seller.

Culpeper, as a believer in astrology, describes the government and virtues of the herbs. Of agrimony he goes on to say, "It is an herb under Jupiter and the sign Cancer; and strengthens those parts under the planet and sign, and removes diseases in them by sympathy. . . It openeth and cleanseth the liver, helpeth the jaundice, and is very beneficial to the bowels, healing all inward wounds, bruises, hurts and other distempers."

Agrimony is not native to America, but the seeds were probably brought to this country by the early settlers. Surprisingly, it is a member of the Rosaceae family. The same family as our garden roses.

My 1987 *Rodale's Illustrated Encyclopedia of Herbs* still ascribes medicinal properties to agrimony. For minor ailments such as a sore throat or mouth, "try gargling with an infusion of agrimony. Agrimony tea has been drunk to alleviate coughs and to clear skin eruptions. John Lust, author of *The Herb Book*, recommends that you make an infusion from 2 to 4 teaspoons of the dried leaves with one cup of water and drink a cup a day."

As for its safety, Rodale's book says, "James Duke, Ph.D., a botanist with the U.S. Department of Agriculture, rates this herb as safe as coffee, stating that he wouldn't be afraid to drink 2 cups a day."

I gathered some to dry. I may need it this winter.

My old back was beginning to ache from all the bending over. With the raspberries I had picked and frozen earlier, I had enough for our jam. There will be more berries ripening if the weather holds.

I stopped at the Old Sea Dog's Hobby House, where he is making a case for his beautiful model of the Constitution. He is sanding. I gave him the best berry in the bucket and he picked the agrimony burs off my sleeve and back. It was time for lunch.

The Best Things in Life are Free

The weather held, and several days later I returned to our raspberry patch. We were having company for dinner, and what better desert than fresh wild raspberries with cream.

There were still lots of berries, so I picked selectively. This time I ate the half berries, and kept only the nice ones.

This week the mosquitoes were out, with their annoying whine. It was warm, and I didn't have on long sleeves. I have a welt or two to show for my hour. In that time I picked two cups, enough for four nice servings.

While I was picking, I thought what a shame it was that my great-grand-children couldn't be with me. Years ago, when my grandchildren were small, I took them picking. Usually, their pail bottoms would be scarcely covered, and those berries would still have stems. Little beatles, worms, sticks, and burs would be amongst the broken fruit. They ate the best ones.

It was then that we would get out the jam recipe of our lake neighbor, Mrs. Harris. Perhaps you would like to try it, when there are too few berries and too many people.

Children's Jam

Crush and measure your wild raspberries, preferably picked by children or grandchildren, but picked over and cleaned by an adult. Add an equal quantity of sugar.

Slowly bring to a boil, and then cook over high heat, stirring constantly for about ten minutes. If the children are old enough, they can help stir. Sterilize one, or more peanut butter jars and lids. Fill. There is no need for paraffin. It won't last.

The adults prefer my cordial. This is a recipe that I saw years ago in *Gourmet*. I have made it every year, both with raspberries and blackberries.

Cordial

3 cups of berries

1 1/2 cups sugar

Cook 40 minutes in top of double-boiler. Strain through cheese cloth. You should have 1 1/2 cups of juice. Cool. Add:

1 cup brandy

1 1/2 cups vodka

Wait at least a week. The natural pectin will thicken this somewhat. The blackberry is especially good for an upset stomach. Yum.

A delicious herbal tea can be made of raspberry, blackberry, or strawberry leaves. Dry thoroughly, crush and store in glass jars. Use as you would any tea.

Because of my column, friends have been asking me about the flowers on the roadside. I am not a botanist, only a hobbyist, and my memory is beginning to go. At the Iron County Museum in Caspian, Michigan, Jean Lindbeck had made a beautiful large basket arrangement for our Italian Day celebration. It was of Queen Anne's Lace and the lovely lavender flowers that grow so profusely along our county roads. The name for the lavender flowers just wouldn't come to mind. I could hardly wait to get home and look it up.

It is knapweed, and I hope I remember it next year. It is related to Bachelor's-button.

This week I saw a rare sight. An animal crossed the county road about a half mile from our home. At first glance, I thought it was a very large squirrel, but its graceful, bounding run and beautiful yellowish brown color and bushy tail told me that it was a pine marten. I had never seen one that close before, but have studied pictures of these wilderness animals.

According to my old, well worn booklet, *Michigan Wildlife Sketches*, by G. W. Bradt, and the Education Department of the Michigan Department of Conservation, 1950, this member of the weasel family cannot withstand the encroachment of civilization. They prefer coniferous forests.

The marten is the number one enemy of the squirrel. He can streak through the trees, and leap as far or farther than any squirrel.

In Victor Cahalane's book, *Mammals of North America*, he tells the following story.

"At least one mallard duck took a marten 'for a ride.' He had been captured by the marten and dragged about forty feet toward a clump of firs. But the drake didn't give up. Struggling valiantly, he carried the marten off the ground and into the air several times. Each time the marten pulled him back to earth. Once the mallard carried it thirty feet. But at last the duck was killed, and the marten carried him into a hole under the trees and devoured him."

This was also the week of the Perseid meteor shower. We were fortunate to have a beautiful night. The Old Sea Dog, his sister and I, took a torch and walked to the center of our field. From there we had a clear view of the northeastern sky.

The O.S.D. pointed out the stars that he used to use for navigation. I found the few constellations that I remembered from camp; Ursa major, Ursa minor, (the big and little dipper), polaris, (the north star), and the "M" shaped Cassiopeia. The milky way spread its way across the sky.

We had hardly arrived when the show began. Perhaps the meteors weren't as frequent as fourth of July fireworks, but they were awe inspiring. They were so rapid that it was difficult to finish a wish before they were gone.

The papers reported that many people made long trips to get far enough away from city lights to view this phenomena.

Florists are paid huge sums for flower arrangements as lovely as Jean's.

People spend thousands of dollars to go on wilderness trips to see wild animals.

We have it all, and it's free!

Mushrooms, Eat
with Caution!

I t is hard to remember how hot and humid it was last week, how hazy and muggy. The mornings were foggy and the fields covered with mist.

During the night the grass spiders painted our old pasture with their funnel webs. Each morning, the grass was festooned with gossamer doilies, embroidered with drops of pearly dew.

The spider's funnel webs stretch horizontally between blades of grass, each web varying from the size of a saucer to a dinner-plate. Like their name, they are concave with a narrow downward hallway of retreat; the hiding place of the builder. You won't catch her, because she has a rear exit.

The grass spider's web is so sheer that each blade of grass or weed can be seen through it. When I touched one, it dissolved beneath my finger, leaving my finger damp.

Late yesterday afternoon we had a torrential downpour. It was over in less than an hour, leaving the air fresh and cool. After dinner we went for our walk, Down Our Road. That evening we were joined by our neighbor and her two chocolate labs.

In the wet muddy road, the deer tracks were everywhere. We must have at least six resident does and fawns in our field and woods. They have a well worn path that cuts down a slope from the road and crosses where there are the fewest rocks. From looking at their tracks, they must have had a barn dance on the road to celebrate the rain. Even the largest doe must have been jumping for joy. The hoof marks were deep and sashayed every-which-way.

The dogs were glad to be out, and their tracks went through the puddles, ours around.

The air was cooler than the field, and the fog was rolling across it. Where the road dips, we got a cool bath. It was a relief after the heat of the day.

There were the early signs of the coming fall. The fall asters in bloom, the milkweed pods beginning to form, and the thistle seeds showing their down.

This is the time for the American goldfinch to leave the flock and pair off for nesting. The male is at his brightest yellow, with his contrasting black forehead, wings and tail. The female is olive-green, lighter below, with a white rump. Goldfinch depend on the milkweed or thistle-down to line their tightly woven nests, and the thistle seeds to feed their young. The adults regurgitate the seeds to feed the babies.

On our way back, I decided to look where the shaggy mane mushrooms grow. None yet, but better than that, there was a giant puffball, Calvatia gigantea! The beach-ball like growth was fastened by only a small "root", with no stalk. It wasn't the biggest one I've ever seen, but when I measured it later I found it was 21 inches in circumference.

Our friend had never seen one before, but she loves mushrooms. We stopped at her house, and I cut it in half. Under the thick rind, was a solid core of white. It smelled so wonderful.

To be edible it must always have solid white flesh, not yellow, slimy or wormy, and with no signs of an interior stalk. Look it up in a mushroom book. However, once seen, it is one of the easiest to identify.

We had hardly gotten home, when the phone rang. Our mushroom loving friend had sauteed a couple of slices and pronounced it as "good as caviar."

The next afternoon, the doorbell rang. Our neighbor stood at our door holding two large, stark white mushrooms. I screamed, "Throw those away, and come in here and wash your hands right away." She was holding Amanita verna, destroying angel. The smaller one had the vulva, cup-like base and was still in the round button shape. The larger parasol one had a prominent veil around the stalk. It was beautiful, therefore double dangerous.

In 1986, the Boss and I had attended a mushroom workshop given by the extension service of Michigan Technological University. It was taught by Dr. Johann N. Bruhn. Several years later, he was one of the discoverers of the 1,500-year-old Armillaria mellea mushroom that covers over thirty seven acres south of Crystal Falls, in Michigan's Upper Peninsula. Locally this fungus has come to be called the "Humungous Fungus." A yearly fall festival is celebrated in its honor with a mushroom cook-off held at the local museum.

At Dr. Bruhn's seminar we learned to be extremely cautious with mushrooms.

Some of his rules of collecting are:

1. Don't eat unknown mushrooms raw, or even nibble and spit.
2. Bag species individually, preferably in paper bags.
3. Learn one species at a time, identify with certainty.
4. Cook only one kind at a time. Save a couple of specimens in the refrigerator for identification in case of poisoning.
5. Watch for allergies. Some people are allergic to mushrooms that others can eat without problems.

There are many good mushroom guides. Michigan State University has fine mushroom booklets for sale at a nominal price through their County Cooperative Extension Service. One is entitled, "Don't Pick Poison." I recommend it to all.

Last night, we had company for dinner, and I served our half of the puffball. With two slices each, I still had enough for the next nights dinner. It was delicious.

But caution and knowledge are the key words. DON'T PICK POISON.

The Virtues of Weeds

It was time to mow the lawn for the last time this season. At least the Old Sea Dog hopes it will be the last time.

Did I say "lawn"? Lawn brings up memories of lush grass, neatly trimmed.

Ours is not a lawn. Perhaps yard is a better word. It gets as little care as possible. We believe in laissez faire, "noninterference in the life of others," except for the regular cutting.

Lush grass? Not our rocky yard. My mother called our place Boulder Knob. Underneath our soil are the rocks that the glacier left behind. The only thing that will grow well on our waste ground are weeds!

What is a definition of "weeds"?

In the book, *Weeds*, by Walter Conrad Muenscher, he says: "The word 'weed' suggests a useless, ugly or harmful plant that persists in growing where it is not wanted. Many weeds possess one or more, but not necessarily all, of these characteristics. A plant may be useful, beautiful or harmless and still be a weed under certain conditions. Weeds are those plants, with harmful or objectionable habits or characteristics, which grow where they are not wanted, usually in places where it is desired that something else should grow."

Are the plants in our yard weeds? Others might think so, but if grass cannot survive around our house, then those green plants that will, are more than welcome.

Ralph Waldo Emerson wrote in one of his essays, "What is a weed? A plant whose virtues have not yet been discovered."

We do have one kind of grass, crab grass. It fills in between the orange hawkweed, chickweed, black mustard, dandelions, prunella, pineapple weed, and plantain.

Chickweed is supposed to taste like spinach. I must admit that I've never tried it. It would take a quart or two to make a serving.

Dandelions, when young are very tasty. I like them in a salad with a hot dressing of bacon fat, vinegar, and sugar with bits of crisp bacon and onion. But not at this time of year or under our present dietary rules!

Pineapple weed is a cousin of chamomile. You can spot it by its rayless disk flowers. It is small, erect, much branched with finely cut leaves. When you crush it, it gives forth the wonderful smell of pineapple. It may not have all the attributes of Peter Rabbit's mother's chamomile, but it makes a very good tea. The *Peterson's Field Guide to Edible Wild Plants*, says, "Excellent."

I dry it for winter.

The orange hawkweed, Hieracium aurantiacum, is probably the one with the least value. Except that it is beautiful in a field of ox-eye daisies, and goldenrod. It is mildly fragrant and is loved by bees and small butterflies, but it doesn't keep well in a bouquet.

Two of my books call it such a troublesome weed in fields and pastures that some counties have laws for its eradication.

The 17th century herbalist, Nicholas Culpeper, cites many medicinal uses for hawkweed, but his identification is hazy. In more modern herbals orange hawkweed is not listed. A member of the same family, mouse-ear is given credit for reputedly curing liver ailments, diarrhea, asthma, nosebleeds, etc. I don't plan to try it.

What I do use, and use often is plantain. Plantain is everywhere. It was brought to the new world by the earliest settlers. The Indians are said to have called it Englishman's foot, but they soon used it as their own.

There are three species and all can be used in the same manner. The common plantain, Plantago major, is the one found most often in the north country. It has a rosette of broad oval leaves. The seed spikes are greenish white, and may reach 2 feet. Look it up at the library if you don't have an herbal; it is invaluable.

A friend of mine's daughter sat on a needle, which broke off in her leg. It became festered and the child was in pain. Her mother called the doctor who told her to come in the next day if it wasn't any better and he would probe for the point.

"What do you have to lose," I told her. "Try this plantain leaf tonight."

The pain left, the swelling came to a head, and the needle point came out by itself.

More recently, an acquaintance burned herself on the hand and was in a lot of pain. I got her a plantain leaf, washed it off, and bandaged it on. It removed the pain almost immediately.

I sound like the old medicine men.

"Tell you what this plant will do. This 'mother of herbs' is an astringent, will stop bleeding, is a remedy for cuts, sores, burns, snake and insect bites. Not only that, but tea from the seeds are a remedy for diarrhea, dysentery, and bleeding from mucous membranes. What will you give me for this plant? Not five dollars, not two dollars, but free! Step right outside and pick it for yourself."

This week O.S.D. decided to re-waterproof our deck. First, he had to remove the encroaching crown vetch and snow-on-the-mountain. We had planted both. Three wheelbarrows full and several hours later he was ready to paint. Now those are WEEDS.

Signs That
Our Summer's Leaving

The small signs of fall are everywhere. The maple leaves are changing; the fall aster and goldenrod are fading; the Queen Anne's lace has turned into bird's nests; and the fireweed's seed pods are bursting open.

The fireweed is a member of the primrose family and was given its name because they are often the first flowers to reclaim burned over land; but I like to think they are called fireweed because their downy seeds look like smoke rising from the fields.

Another sure sign that summer is leaving is the beginning of the fall migration of our summer birds.

Last week a small male ruby-throated hummingbird flew into our garage and zoomed around the Old Sea Dog's head as he worked. These tiny birds know who fills their feeder, and when it is empty they come to our window, peer in, while beating their little wings with the incredible speed of 70 beats per second. They have trained us well. This time the feeder was full. What did he want? Later that day we noticed that all the male hummingbirds had disappeared. Could he have come to say good-bye?

The females are still here, fattening up their young-ones for their long trek south. Our feeders are humming from morning to night, and I'm kept busy refilling them with artificial nectar. (One part sugar, and four parts water) Soon they too will be leaving. Last year it was the first week of September. We'll miss them.

A couple of evenings later, we were driving towards Gaastra on County Road 424. Just before we got to Olsen's farm the sky was filled with hundreds of birds darting this way and that, soaring, and diving. They were as large as a blue jay, but with long pointed, inverted V-shaped wings. We slowed down and I was able to see the large white patches under the wings. They were nighthawks, gathering their evening meal of night flying insects. Their name is misleading, as they are neither hawks nor totally nocturnal. They are members of the goatsucker family, named for the European myth that they sucked the milk of goats. They are a cousin of the Whip-poor-will, and on the ground or sitting cross-ways on a branch, they look much alike. The car windows were open and we could hear their nonmusical "bee-ak".

Nighthawks are also called nightjars because of the peculiar vibrating, booming noise that they sometimes make with their wings, as they fly. This has been likened to the sound of "a strong wind blowing into the bung-hole of an empty barrel."

These nighthawks, like many migrants were gathering together in flocks to start their yearly trip south.

All too soon the Canada geese will be filling our sky. It always makes me sad to see them, and our summer go.

We have had more hot, sticky days, during the approaching fall than we've had all summer. Usually by late afternoon the clouds form and a cool breeze sets in from the north, so after the dinner dishes, we go for our evening walk.

Our walks start easily, from our house on the hill. Going down is never a problem. The struggle is on the return.

I must be an oral person, for even though I've had my dinner, I like to nibble my way down the hill.

At this time of year my favorite munch is peppergrass, Lepidium virginicum, sometimes called poorman's pepper. Earlier in the summer, the tiny four petaled white flowers form a cross, giving the name Cruciferae to this and all other members of the mustard family.

Peppergrass is described in Fernald and Kinsey's book, *Edible Wild Plants of Eastern North America*, as "leaves in spring forming rosettes, the individual leaves deeply cut or toothed and with the characteristic cress flavor; flowers minute, white or whitish, in elongating slender spike-like clusters, with 4 petals (these sometimes wanting) in opposite pairs; seed-pod flat, circular or nearly so, notched at the summit."

The young shoots make a good substitute for water-cress, and the peppery seed pods are good in salads or soups as seasoning. I just like to strip off the small seeds with my teeth and chew them as I walk.

The chokecherries are black and juicy. They are an acquired taste, usually developed as a child. Even the best of them pucker your mouth, but I like one or two.

Subconsciously, as I walk along, I pull out the top portion of grasses, from inside their sheath. This is another habit of childhood. I enjoy the taste of the tender white tips.

Sometimes our good neighbor walks with us. He and the O.S.D. have been known to make projectiles of the grasses, such as timothy or fox grass, and they have spur-of-the-moment contests to see whose spear goes the furthest. They are adept at throwing them for quite a distance. I eat, they throw.

We reach the mailboxes. The Jack-in-the-pulpit at the corner has formed its beautiful fiery red seed cluster. Another sign of the approach of fall.

We make our swing to return the half mile to the house. Half way back, we start our climb; a climb which a few years ago was no problem. My concentration is on getting to the top. No more nibbles on the way back.

Fall

Escape to a
Silent Hemlock Forest

*T*his is the week that the Master Mariner became the "master plumber." The thirty-five year old trap elbow of the kitchen sink sprang a leak.

Although he has done plumbing before, once putting in a whole bathroom on a third floor, he was reluctant to try this. It involved taking out a disposal, and working under the sink with badly corroded pipes, and the builder hadn't put in shut-off valves.

He called a plumber, too busy, "try so and so." Same answer, "not for a couple of days."

"I'll have to do it myself, but I'll save money," was his reluctant conclusion. Soon the air was filled with blue smoke. I went for a walk, leaving the Old Sea Dog to his fate.

Fortunately the weather had cleared, and the sun came out. A gorgeous cool, early fall afternoon. I headed for my favorite trail along the lake.

A nuthatch was giving his "yank, yank" from somewhere in the woods. The sun shone on the sumac leaves, already scarlet, above the golden brown bracken. A late purple clover caught my eye, and I was soon nibbling the sweet white tips.

A gray squirrel scurried up an enormous oak at the side of the road and out on one of the topmost branches, dropping to a smaller tree on the other side of the road. His aerial path called my attention to the fact that in a year or two this beautiful old tree would be gone. The decay was already evident with several large woodpecker holes, and fungus growing from some of the broken branches. One of the holes was probably the squirrel's home or perhaps the home of the raccoons that my neighbor has been complaining about.

At first I thought that the large white growth on the side of the tree was the delicious oyster mushroom, but on closer examination I saw that it was a mass of overlapping toothed layers. It wasn't stiff like a polypore or bracket fungi.

From long habit, I always carry a small bag for any treasures. I broke off a sample to take home for identification and popped it into my bag.*

A blue jay sounded his rusty gate call, telling all in that part of the woods that a stranger had entered their territory. Soon a whole flock were squawking my presence, flying from tree to tree.

Overhead I heard a more important sound. In the spring, I rejoice to hear the honking and chattering, but in the fall the call of the Canada geese heading South makes me sad. I counted thirty four, changing patterns, and reforming to allow another leader to take his place at the head of the arrow formation. The weather man had predicted a clear cold night, and the birds had read the same signs.

The lake shimmered in the sun. Somewhere on the other shore I heard a single shot. Had a bear met his end, or had the hunter missed? It was quiet again, except for the jays.

As I always do, I examined the plants at the water's edge. The wild mint (Mentha arvensis) grows in profusion here. It still had some of its tiny blossoms clustered in circles at the junction of the leaf stalks. I tasted it, but it was very strong. I love the smell. It is our only native mint.

(*Later I was able to identify it as Hericium erinaceus, Latin for porcupine. A white porcupine?)

A few plants of arrowhead, Sagittaria latifolia, had their tubers rooted in the water. They are sometimes called wappato, the name that Lewis and Clark learned from the Chinook Indians of the Pacific Northwest. The one inch to two inch milky tubers have been used as food by the natives for centuries. They are unpleasant raw, but are said to taste like a potato when boiled or roasted. If I were younger, or if it were a warm summer day, I would take off my shoes and socks and tread them out the way the Indians did. But it would take a lot to make a meal. Perhaps I'll try it someday.

The jewelweed has finished blooming and its explosive seed pods have dispersed their seeds. The seed pods give it its other common name, touch-me-not. Its watery stem is useful for taking the sting from nettles or as a quick first aid if you know you've gotten into poison ivy.

The wild plum trees have fruit for the first time in years, but they are not ripe. A sample goes in my bag along with the mint.

A few yards on I enter the path that has been here for centuries. My father and others have told me that it was an Indian trail before it became a wagon road.

Fallen logs along the trail are covered with mosses of many kinds. I gather a few to look at under a lens. In the spring Clintonia and pink lady slippers grow here. The Clintonia's blue seeds are gone as are the leaves of the orchid.

I pass the tiny beach where our youngest son used to play with the neighbor boy, building sand castles and leaving notes to each other on birch bark. That was so long ago.

At last I enter the cathedral of ancient hemlock. The jays have decided that I'm no longer a threat, and all is still. The sun filters through the trees making patterns on the path — a place of peace and prayer — a prayer that the plumber hasn't run into too much trouble.

I hate to leave this enchanted place, for I probably will not return until spring.

On the way back, I pick up a fallen transparent apple and enjoy its tart juiciness on the way back up the hill.

Back home, a grimy plumber greets me, the worst is over. He has removed all the necessary parts and will only have to replace the pipes.

I'm still washing dishes in the bathroom for a few days more. But, my Master Mariner has promised that we'll go out to dinner with the money he saved because no master plumber would come. With the prices of plumbers, he'll probably have money left over for a new tool, and maybe, there will even be enough for another reference book for the First Mate.

A Time to Gather

Breakfast was over, but I was still gathering myself together for the day ahead and sipping my morning coffee. Our kitchen window looks out over the mixed stand of conifers that my mother and father planted in 1959.

Although it was early, an energetic red squirrel was bouncing across the drive with something in his mouth. He appeared to have an upward curving horn coming out of his head. On closer look, I saw that it was a large green pine cone. He headed for the base of "his" tree where he stashed it. Back and forth he went. Up the white pine; out on a high limb; and out to the furthest branches where the cones were forming; there he'd gnaw at a cone; tug on the cone, shake the whole branch; secure the cone, dash down the tree; and scurry to "his" storehouse. Back and forth, up and down. He made me tired.

He is a noisy little fellow. Intruders get told off with repetitious "Tch-Wunk, Tch-Wunk."

Of course, he has found the way onto our feeder. We beat on the window with a fly-swatter, but he won't move until we start to open the window, then he'll take a flying leap to the deck fifteen feet below. It doesn't seem to hurt him any, as he is back again when our backs are turned.

Last winter in an effort to keep the squirrels off our feeders, we would toss peanuts to them. At first they didn't know what they were. The gray squirrels would bury them in the snow. But after we cracked a few shells the red squirrels learned to sit and enjoy them.

One warm day when we had the windows open by the feeders, we came into the living room to find one of the red rascals sitting on top of our seed storage box munching a peanut from the paper bag. He had chewed a two inch hole in our plastic screen. We had visions of chasing him through the house, but our presence sent him scurrying out the way he came. The Old Sea Dog had to replace the screens, this time with steel mesh.

In spite of all this we find them entertaining and admire their persistence.

We had company from the BIG CITY during August. She loves to watch the animals. The O.S.D. bought some dried corn on the cob and wired it to a pole. It was better than a movie. First the chipmunk found it. He really had to stretch to remove the kernels. One small fellow managed to stuff about ten of the seeds into his cheek pouches. Finally when he couldn't get another one in, he scampered off to his home under the rocks.

The red squirrel was next. He too had to stretch to reach the seeds. After trying many positions he found it was easier to hang upside down on the cob, where he chewed and chattered at the returning chippie.

The final visitor was the gray squirrel, who somehow managed to make off with the whole cob.

We have still one more squirrel that we enjoy seeing. Almost every evening about nine we hear a little thump on the feeder. Our flying squirrel has come for his supper.

He turns his back on our light, and drapes his flat tail over the edge of the feeder. He is tiny, and weighs only three to five ounces. He is misnamed as he doesn't fly, but glides from tree to tree.

According to Victor Cahalane in *Mammals of North America*, when the flying squirrel takes great leaps into space it "immediately spreads out all four legs at right angles to its body. This stretches out the 'wings' which are folds of skin covered with fine, close-lying fur."

"The air, rushing by underneath, bows the skin of the 'wings' upward. Deftly the squirrel sails downward through the air for one hundred and fifty feet, or twice as far if it takes advantage of sloping ground."

By twisting and turning and steering with his tail he can control his course and speed.

Most of us don't even know that he is around, but he too has begun his winter gathering of nuts and seeds.

As I write, two gray squirrels are running up our oak tree. This year we have a large crop of acorns. Does this mean a severe winter?

It isn't only the squirrels who have been gathering. When I stepped outside I could hear the sound of a chain saw across the lake. Someone is making wood for the winter to come.

My good friend will soon be migrating south again. To reminder her of her beloved northern woods, I went gathering. With a pair of hedge clippers, I clipped the overhanging tips of some of our balsam firs.

With a scrap of heavy green twill, I cut a piece about 10 inches by 5 inches, folded it in half with right sides together, and stitched up two sides. Then I turned it right-side out and stuffed it with the soft balsam tips, and finished off the open end.

There I had it, a quick inexpensive gift of the northwoods. The wonderful odor will remain for years. I have one that I made over fifteen years ago, and when it is squeezed it still smells piney.

This could be an easy gift for a child to make for a grandparent. I once had my Nature Workshop kids make them. They were quite young, so I pre-sewed the two sides. It was a craft they enjoyed.

I don't have a garden to harvest, but I have gathered and dried my herbal teas, and my pods, flowers, and grasses. When the snows are on the ground, I'll sit and sip my tea, admire my dried arrangements, and sniff my balsam pillow.

Harvest Time Hayride and Other Joys of Fall

*T*he Old Sea Dog and I hadn't gone on a hayride for almost 60 years. This time the horses were replaced by a modern tractor, and instead of giggling teen-agers, the riders were of all ages.

A young couple invited us to a harvest party and celebration of their new farm home. The weather cooperated and although it was cool we could eat the fabulous roast lamb, and potluck supper out-of-doors.

Their new home is almost finished, a deck and porch are all that is needed to complete the outside. We were impressed with the house. They did much of the work themselves with the help of family. Good Yupper hard work.

The farm itself was a scene from *Country Magazine*. The red and gold maples gleamed in the sun in a wood behind a large barn. A field of golden grass held grazing horses. One guest was leaning over the fence stroking the nose of a lovely black mare with a white blaze. In the foreground were a hay wagon, dogs, a barn cat, and children jumping and rolling in piles of hay.

After we could eat no more, our host pulled up the tractor with the large hay wagon. A double row of bales were our seats. Grandmothers, grandfathers and great grandparents like the O.S.D. and I were pushed and pulled aboard (I must admit that I had difficulty). The young parents, toddlers, and younger children clambered on, and we were off down the country road.

At first we rode alongside of fields with herds of cows and an occasional farm house. Around a bend the next field held five grazing deer. They didn't even look up as we passed.

An occasional car would squeeze by.

It wasn't long before we left the last house. The road narrowed, becoming a dirt trail with wetlands on both sides. Green hummocks of moss rose up amid the puddles. Tag alder made up most of the underbrush. Overhead, branches kept scrapping the uprights on the wagon. Several times we had to duck. The wagon lurched and bumped, but that was part of the fun.

At the bottom of the hill we made a difficult turn onto a logging road. Between the trees an abandoned tractor was rotting along with the slashings. I hope the owner will return to salvage it.

A fox ran across the logged hill. Before I could finish saying, "There's a fox," he was gone.

We passed some empty summer cabins, and soon came to a small lake covered with water lilies where the DNR have built a small park and a boat landing.

The young ones piled out. A late summer yarrow was picked and proclaimed, "Queen Anne's lace." Of course, "Old Know It All" had to correct them. But it was neither the time nor place to give the history of yarrow. Its Latin name is Achillea millefolium, named for the Greek hero, Achilles who is said to have given yarrow to his soldiers to staunch their wounds. The stiff stems are used by the Chinese in the casting of fortunes through the *I Ching, the Book of Changes*. For us, they make a good addition to a dried bouquet.

After the short stop we were again on the country road, bouncing back toward the house. The sun was just beginning to set as the tractor turned into the farm. Red streaks across the western sky brought an end to a wonderful autumn day.

We felt fortunate to have been included with these friends and their family.

Today the sun stayed out long enough for the O.S.D. to finish staining our deck with water repellent for the winter ahead. I should get out the apple picker and visit our many trees.

Last year we had bushels of juicy apples. I dried some. They are a great munch when you are on a diet, as I usually am. I also made a batch of apple jelly, several pies, and we still had too many.

We had company from South Carolina who had never made cider. To tell the truth, neither had we. We borrowed an ancient cider press, and set to work. It was work. Our garage was soon filled with a wonderful apple aroma as we crushed and then squeezed the pulp. We finally got about five gallons of juice.

The O.S.D. thought it was too mild, and read up on making hard cider.

By freezing the juice, and pouring off the unfrozen portion, he finally got a little zing. But you can tell he really didn't think much of it, as we still have some in the refrigerator.

This year our apples are late, small, and not as juicy. We won't be borrowing the press.

Our youngest son and his wife are coming for a visit and I'll make apple pies — one of October's blessings.

The Unusual Life of the Lichens

*L*ittle did I know what I was getting into when I brought home samples of interesting mosses to identify. I got out my plant guides and began searching for names of the charming little funnel shaped cups, tiny towers, and swan neck growths atop thin filaments that I had found among the green clusters.

Much to my surprise, only one was a moss, the one with the swan neck. It was a woodsy Mnium, or star moss (Mnium cuspidatum). Don't ask me how that's pronounced. The others were not mosses at all, but lichens. I had always thought of lichens as those gray growths on rocks, branches, and old fences.

The funnel shaped ones are called pyxie cups (Cladonia pyxidata). They look like fairies' pewter goblets.

The tiny towers were aptly named, ladder lichen (Cladonia verticillata). When I got out my high powered magnifying glass I could appreciate their symmetry. Each funnel shaped cup rose from the center of the one below it. The rims of the funnels were edged in red.

I turned to an encyclopedia to learn that lichens are a combination of two distinct species, an alga (a primitive aquatic plant) and a fungus. The algae, which can photosynthesize, contributes food; the fungi furnish water and shade. Lichens are one of the best illustrations of symbiosis (living together) as the scientists call this intimate relationship of two different kinds of organisms.

The fungus makes the bulk of the body with its interwoven threads, and in the meshes of the threads live the algae. Lichens can grow under the most adverse conditions, scorching deserts, and Arctic tundra.

Why had it never registered that they were such amazing plants? Did I sleep through high-school biology?

At the library I found *Forests of Lilliput, The Realm of Mosses and Lichens* by John Bland. At first I thought it was more than I wanted to know about these flowerless plants.

After reading a few pages, I found it consoling that distinguished lichenologists disagree about classification of certain mosses and lichens. If a plant is called a moss it isn't always so. Sea moss is an algae. The clubmosses (ground pines, running pines, or princess pine as it's called in the U.P.) are descendants of the ancient clubmoss trees of the Paleozoic Era. The reindeer moss is a lichen, and so is that delicate food for invalids, Iceland-moss.

No wonder a poor hobbyist is confused.

As an aside, the princess pine is protected in Michigan. Too many people ripped it from the forest floor to make Christmas decorations. It is not endangered yet, but is illegal to pick on State land.

Bland's book, once he got past the scientific material, turned out to be full of fascinating lore.

Lichens have been eaten by man and beast since the beginning of time. In Lapland, reindeer eat the "moss" named for them during the severe winters. Lichens are a human survival food throughout the world. They contain starch and even some vitamin C. One species of lichen are made into the "earth bread" of the Tartars.

A desert species is named Manna lichen. Bland says that some scientists feel that lichens were the manna of the bible. See Numbers XI: 7-9. In recent times there have been reports that when hail melted, following a violent storm, the ground was covered with lichen. Scientists tested them and declared them edible.

As early as the sixteenth century lichens were used in the perfume and cosmetic industry. The plants were dried, ground and combined with other ingredients including ambergris (a secretion of the sperm-whale's intestine) musk, and oil of roses to produce the most expensive products.

Oak "moss," another lichen, is still used in the perfume business. It is said to harmonize with the other ingredients and give stability.

Lichens are used for sizing paper, in gums, mucilage, gelatin and isinglass.

But most interesting (to me) is their use in the dye industry. According to Bland, about 1300 A.D. a Florentine "rediscovered the method of preparation and use of the Rocella dye . . . he noted that urine (very likely his own, as he relieved himself on a Mediterranean beach) imparted a fine purple-blue color to certain lichens. Experimenting successfully, he founded a very lucrative dye industry."

The use of human urine was commonplace in the dye industry from that time on, being the only early source of ammonia. This use of lichens continued until World War II in Ireland in the making of Harris Tweeds.

Chemist's litmus paper, that test the alkalinity or acidity of a solution, is made from lichens. Acid turns the paper red, alkalies turn it blue.

Anytime man finds starchy foods, he tries to ferment it to make alcohol. Lichen beer and lichen brandy have been successfully produced.

These insignificant little plants are everywhere, yet we rarely notice them.

Yesterday was beautiful and I took my camera out to photograph mosses and lichens. Only a few feet from the house and growing alongside a clump of moss on a large rock, was the beautiful British soldiers lichen. Its scarlet tips on lumpy gray stalks became a picture that I hope turns out. Surprises are everywhere, when I look.

Myths and Legends of the Wolf

At the September meeting of the Lee LeBlanc Audubon Chapter of Iron County, Michigan, young Evan Premo showed the group his treasure. He carefully unwrapped a relief cast of the track of a large wolf. The paw print was about 5 1/2 inches long and 4 inches wide. He and his father, Dr. Dean Premo, had gone about three miles north of Amasa to the place where Evan's grandfather had seen a large wolf cross the forest road. There they had found the tracks and made the plaster cast.

I have seen the wolf that is on exhibit at the Sylvania Wild Life Center in Watersmeet. It was reported to have been killed in Iron County by a car. I have read about the return of the wolves to Iron and Dickinson County, but this wolf print brought home to me that we live in a wilderness area. We see fisher, marten, mink, bobcat, bear, fox, and loon, but somehow the wolf means the true wild.

October 17th through the 23rd, 1993, was Wolf Awareness Week. On that year's posters, given out through the D.N.R., there was a quote from Sigurd F. Olson, the popular Minnesota wildlife writer, that expresses what I feel.

> "There was real satisfaction in knowing the wolves were in the country and that it was wild and still big enough to roam . . . I wonder if the day would ever come when we would understand the importance of wolves."

Through the centuries humans have had a love/hate relationship with the wolves. Hate coming from fear of their size, ability to kill cattle and sheep, and elusiveness. Love, coming from admiration of their ability to survive, their family unit, and the myths about them.

In Britain, the King of Wales, Edgar the Peaceful (959-975), paid a bounty yearly for 300 wolves. After three years, the bounty could not be filled. There are no records of wolves in England after the 15th Century, but a few were recorded in Ireland and Scotland until the 18th century.

In Greek mythology, it was said that the priests of Zeus could take the form of a wolf. In Scandinavian legend, the Fenris Wolf is a force of terror and destruction. In Germany the wolf is associated with the devil. Witches were said to take the shape of wolves.

The New Testament has a reference to false prophets as wolves dressed up in sheep's clothing (Matthew 7:15), pointing out the belief that wolves are crafty and malicious.

We have many expressions that express our fear of the wolf. The "wolf pack," a group of German submarines in World War II; "to keep the wolf from the door," to ward off starvation; and "thrown to the wolves," to be sacrificed.

I was raised with the stories of "The Boy Who Cried Wolf," "The Three Little Pigs," and "Little Red Riding Hood." All stories where the wolf was the enemy.

But, I was also raised with stories of the good wolves. One of my favorite books was *The Jungle Book* by Rudyard Kipling. He told of the Indian baby, Mowgli, who wandered into the wolves den, and was adopted and suckled by the she wolf. Last night I got out my father's well-worn copy and reread about how Mowgli finally killed Shere Khan, the tiger, with the help of his wolf "brothers." I still find it exciting.

The Aztecs had a story of twins being suckled by a wolf mother, very reminiscent of Romulus and Remus in Roman mythology. It is probably from these stories that Rudyard Kipling took his idea for Mowgli.

There is also the Christian legend of St. Francis of Assisi and the wolf of Gubbio. St. Francis is said to have reproved the wolf, who was terrorizing the countryside, and after that, the wolf lived amicably among the people.

My children and I enjoyed Farley Mowat's story, *Never Cry Wolf*. It is full of humor, and of Mowat's life near a wolf family during an Alaskan winter. It is a wonderful tale for a reluctant reader.

Our favorite wolf story is a true one. My husband has a Norwegian Sea Captain friend, who got himself in deep trouble with the parents of his six year old daughter's friends, all over a wolf story.

His daughter and her friends had asked him to tell them about his life in Norway when he was a child. He embroidered the hardships, the cold winters, and the times of famine. Then he said, "Before I was born my parents were traveling by horse drawn sleigh across the frozen steppes, when they heard the howls of a pack of wolves. The sound grew louder and louder. Father whipped the horses, but the wolves kept getting closer and closer. Father turned to Mother, 'We may have to throw baby Ingemar to the wolves.' The horses ran faster and faster, but still the wolves got closer and closer until their hot foul, breath could be felt on Mother's neck. 'There is only one thing to do,' Father said, 'Throw the baby, Mother, throw the baby.' While the wolves devoured the baby, my mother and father were able to escape."

The listening children, burst into tears, and ran home. Five minutes later the phone was ringing off the hook.

It is fearful stories like this, that have led to the elimination of the wolf.

Our Upper Peninsula wolves have migrated back from Northern Minnesota and Wisconsin because of our healthy wilderness. They are an endangered species, and killing one is both a State and Federal violation.

I am looking forward to someday hearing a chorus of wolves, howling and barking. Then I'll know that, yes, I do live in a very special place.

The Hunt for
October's Reds

They came for the colors. Their trip from Florida had been planned for the third week of September, but work (that necessity of life) had interfered. We picked them up in Marquette on a bright sunny morning on October 6th.

Already, Iron Counties' scarlets had gone from the maples, but the yellows of the birch, popple, and tamaracks shimmered in the sun. Coming Down Our Road, the overhanging canopy was breathtaking. Our son, the serious photographer, was ecstatic. Our daughter-in-law, the artist, could hardly wait to get out her watercolors.

Then predictably, the clouds came, it got colder, and we had snow flurries. It gave them time to unwind, and for us to catch up on the news. It gave time for the Shutterbug to clean his lenses and decide what he'd photograph, when the light was right.

The next two mornings, the Camera Man was out at sunrise, bundled up in his layers of winter clothes, topped by his photographer's vest, pockets filled with lenses, filters and film. His father's borrowed fur hat finished the picture. The thirty degree weather was a far cry from the 80s they had left in Florida.

We planned everything around the photo-opportunities, and the weather reports. When it was cloudy, drizzling, or we had snow flurries, our youngest helped his father bring in the boat, and cut up wood. His wife and I baked and talked and talked. While I read, she painted scenes from our windows.

On Sunday, the weather man said, "GO". It was time for the annual trip to the Copper Country, and the sun cooperated. It seems strange that north of us the colors were at their peak. It must be that the lake effect had kept off the heavy freeze that we had had earlier.

The sumac was fiery, and the maples were shades of green, yellow and red, all on one tree, and even all on one leaf. The tamarack, or larch, were still green. The bays and lakes were calm and brilliant blue to match the sky. We were drunk with the beauty — plenty of photo-opportunities.

We stopped at an old cemetery near Eagle River. While the photographer recorded overgrown tombstones, I spent the time reading the inscriptions — many from the 1860s. They recorded children who died at six months, old timers born overseas in the early 1800's, and men and boys killed in mine accidents in the Cliff Mine. I copied one inscription:

James Fezzey, aged 19 yrs & 8 mo. Killed at Copper Falls Mine, July 15 AD 1872.

> *"How blest is our brother bereft*
> *of all that could burden his mind.*
> *How easy the soul that has left*
> *this wearisome body behind.*
>
> *This earth is affected no more*
> *with sickness or shaken with pain.*
> *The war in the embers is o'er*
> *and never shall vex him again."*

It was a hard life, in that rugged country.

The next photo session was atop Brockway Mountain. Heavy clouds had started to roll in and much time was spent setting up the tripod in just the right place and waiting for the proper light. Our camera-man was not alone. Everywhere I looked there were other serious photographers.

One man was really serious. He had a large box camera on a heavy duty tripod. With a dark cloth draped over his head and the view finder, he reminded me of a picture of earlier cameramen. All the Shutterbugs in the vicinity gathered around for any pearls of wisdom they could glean from this professional.

More clouds rolled in, and all the interesting shadows disappeared. The photographers folded up their equipment and gave up for the evening.

We drove on to Copper Harbor, and a relaxing fish dinner by the shore. We were not the only ones to have a feast. The Restaurateur also served dinner to flocks of mallard ducks and Canada geese outside our window. We enjoyed watching them lower their landing gear and slide in to the beach, skidding to a halt just before hitting the rocks.

I hoped that they would remember to go South.

It was dusk as we headed back towards Houghton. At this time of year, the road was almost deserted. We slowed down when our lights caught a coyote crossing the road. He paused on the shoulder and let us get a good look at his handsome coat and white vest. In this wilderness he hadn't contracted the mange.

A little further on, two raccoons were racing each other down the center of the road. Our lights sent them scooting off into the underbrush. We had hardly stopped commenting on how cunning they were, when there was something else in the road. This time it was a fox, and we had interrupted his meal of a vole or mouse that he was toying with.

These were photo opportunities that went unrecorded on film, but the wonderful day will always be recorded in our memories.

More Photo-Opportunities

L uck was with us, we had a second day of beautiful sunny weather while our son, the camera buff, and his wife were visiting us from Florida.

We suggested Bond Falls, but the photographer wanted to go to Eagle River, Wisconsin by the back roads. I'm glad we did.

As we turned off from U.S. 2, onto Forest Highway 16, a beautiful adult eagle flew low over the car, his white head and tail gleaming in the sun. Just around the corner, a coyote, the second one in two days, crossed the road.

Our son pulled on to the shoulder, grabbed my tripod, and his camera with the telephoto lens, and was off searching for that special picture.

While we waited in the car, two adult eagles flew overhead. We reasoned that there must be a dead deer somewhere near and that they and the coyote had been feasting.

Our son returned to tell us, "Both eagles settled in a big pine. I think I got some great shots."

Further down the road, there is a county park, beside Little Smoky Lake. It was deserted this day. We all remembered that we had stopped for a picnic here when the children were small. Then, beautiful tall pines dominated the scene. Now, all that's left of those ancient trees are their huge decaying stumps.

The light was right for the photographer, nice shadows on the lake. I spent the time looking at the plants growing along the path near the shore and in the woods.

My find of the day was goldthread, Coptis trifolia. The three leaves look much like the strawberry, only shiny, and evergreen.

On the pages of my old *Wild Flowers* book by Homer House, I have a handwritten note, "The goldthread is so named because of the tangle of fine yellow roots which streak the soil like threads of precious metal. These roots yield a yellow dye. A bitter extract made from them has been used by both Indians and white men as a wash to treat soreness of the mouth (thrush), especially in babies. Decoctions of the plant made by a country housewife have also been used as a spring tonic."

Years ago I chewed on one of the roots to see if it is bitter. Yes, it is.

This, of course, is county land and the goldthread plants are few, so I resist the temptation to dig it up for a terrarium. I know where goldthread grows more plentifully. From May through July it's small white blossoms peek out from the sphagnum moss across our lake.

Sticking out from beneath the fallen brown leaves, I spot some tiny red berries, my old friend, false lily of the valley, Canada mayflower, (Maianthemum canadense). They bloom profusely down our hill by the shore at the same time as the true lily of the valley.

On to Eagle River where we enjoyed a good lunch and some shopping. Our son bought an "Indiana Dohms" leather hat which he liked, but wore self-consciously. His wife found a beautiful hand-carved black walnut otter. She fell in love with it, and knew it would look great on their mantle in Florida. They occasionally see an otter in a stream that runs through their property. She walked away, "too expensive." But before we left town it was in our car. I bought still another book and a beautiful sweater. The Old Sea Dog also made a purchase — a couple of small screws that he was unable to find locally!

By now the afternoon shadows were just right for more photography.

We returned by a different route, newly repaired. Two favorite old white pines have been removed to widen the shoulder. It was probably necessary for safety as the deer were hard to see on this stretch. But I miss the landmark pines' beckoning branches.

Back in Iron County, a small boggy lake caught the cameraman's eye. He made his way to the shore through the thick brush for that photo-opportunity.

"There is rhododendron down there," he told me when he returned. Knowing me, he has brought back a couple of leaves.

He was right about the family, Heath, but not the species. He had found both bog rosemary, and Labrador tea. Their habitat is cold bogs where sphagnum moss grows. Bog rosemary has been known to poison sheep, but Labrador tea was used by pioneers as a tea substitute. Both are fuzzy on the under side of their leaves. Labrador tea's fuzz is brown, bog rosemary's is white, both are evergreen with curled leaf margins. Be careful not to confuse them.

One last photo session. Our youngest pulled the car to a stop near a field. The scene: an expanse of cream colored dead grasses, a hill rising with tiers of trees, all of a size vertically and with a uniformity of golden browns. The angle of the sun and shadows just right for a perfect photo.

When we eventually see the slides from these two beautiful day, we will relive this October again. That is the joy of photography.

Preparations for Winter's Approach

The Old Sea Dog and I go for our walk everyday, weather permitting. Our route is a half mile down the road to the mail boxes and a half mile back up the hill. In the summer we take our exercise after dinner and the dishes, but with winter's approach our walk comes in late afternoon. Today our road is covered with fallen leaves, brought down by last night's wind. I can't resist the temptation to scuff my shoes through them, to smell that unique dry leaf odor, and to hear their crunch. Dried leaves always remind me of the piles that I loved to roll in as a child.

When our boys were small they would make nests of the golden leaves while we raked. Their fun made up for the increased work of re-raking.

Along the road one of our apple trees has shed its leaves, but the bright yellow fruit still hangs from its branches like Christmas ornaments. We picked most of our apples earlier, but these were late to ripen.

The O.S.D. picks one and takes a bite. The earlier freeze hasn't hurt its juicy tartness. We alternate bites on our way down the hill.

On one of the stone walls that line our field, a chipmunk scurries away to his home under the rocks, his mouth full of leaves to line his nest. On that same wall, one of his ancestors chose to scold us as we passed by, only to be scooped up by a passing red shouldered hawk.

I have a fondness for chippies, and hope that this one will take more care.

The Eastern chipmunk, Tamias stroatis. is quite a home builder. His main chamber and bedroom is also a storehouse. He will bring in enough seeds and nuts to last him through the winter, storing them under his bed of leaves, or grasses. If he awakens, he just reaches down, and the food is there. He may also have one or two other storerooms for his grain.

The chipmunk is fastidious, and even has a separate room for his toilet.

He does not hibernate in the same manner as the woodchucks who are already asleep for the winter in our area. He will however, curl up with his heart beat slowing, during a sustained cold spell. But if a warming period comes, he may awaken and venture outside for a little exercise.

From February until the middle of March, on warm days, the male will be out looking for his lady love. By April the little ones arrive, usually four to six in a litter.

Beyond the wall we pass the gate that leads into the field. From here to the county road, there are woods on both sides. The woods are open now. All the lush green bracken, and shrubs are gone with only a patch here and there of still green maidenhair fern, moss covered rocks, and young balsam fir. It is hard to remember the white blanket of trillium that carpeted these woods in May. Any day another white carpet will be spread between these trees.

We reach the mail boxes, and turn to make our way back up the hill, stopping at the apple tree on our way and stuffing our pockets with the fruit.

We have about fifteen apple trees on our land, each with different characteristics. This year one of our best trees with big red tart fruit, had only three apples. That late frost last spring froze the blossoms.

Our pride is a very gnarled old tree on the edge of the hill. The fruit is green with the flesh firm and white. I measured one of the largest ones, 12 1/4 inches around. I have pictures of these apples taken alongside of a ruler. Three of them make a foot. None of our friends can identify the species.

Our property formerly was a Finnish potato farm. Were these apple trees planted or did they just spring up? Except for five together, there seems to be no pattern to their spacing.

I have already made several pies, lots of applesauce, and given them to friends so that they too may make pies and applesauce. Today's apples I will slice and put in my drier, no preservative necessary. They make good gifts for Christmas. My son and his wife are hikers. Dehydrated apples make wonderful trail snacks.

I always keep some for my dieting times with a bowl on the table for nibbles in the evening while I read.

With the coming of more indoor weather, perhaps I'll find time to get out the raspberries I squirreled away in the freezer this summer and finally make the seedless jelly that the Boss likes. While all the kettles are out, I'll make apple jelly too.

Like the chipmunk, we will soon be indoors, except on warm sunny days.

Those **#**@*# Cluster Flies

Flies, flies, flies everywhere! Suck them up in the vacuum, swat them, go to the next window, return and there are as many, or more. The sunny days of fall and winter bring them out of nowhere. It would seem that they spring forth, controlled by a malevolent magician.

I caught one in a glass, gave it a shot of bug juice and looked at it closely with a magnifying lens. I could see the golden hairs on the thorax above the middle pair of legs. When these critters rest on the windows they have the habit of overlapping their wings, making them appear slimmer than the common house fly, Musca domestica. But they seldom rest. They climb up the glass, and when they almost reach the top, they drop, only to start over again.

At night they may fly to a lighted lamp and drive you crazy banging against the shade. I wouldn't recommend swatting them as they are greasy when squashed and make an oily mess.

These are cluster flies, sometimes called lake flies, Pollenia rudis, introduced from Europe, date unknown.

On the recommendation of the DNR, I called "the fly authority," Dr. Richard Merritt at Michigan State University who told me that they lay their eggs on earth worms. When the larva hatch they feed upon their host. As adults they seek the light and warmth of houses or cabins. Cluster flies are

— 48 —

sluggish once they get inside. They are only interested in finding a warm spot to hibernate.

How do they get in? Dr. Merritt reported that they enter the smallest of cracks around windows, through attic vents or roof openings. We are certain that there are no cracks large enough in our house, and although we've watched carefully, we have never caught one in the act of crawling in.

Although they undoubtedly carry germs from their source, they seldom leave the warmth of a sunny window or travel to food. Biologists insist they do not breed inside.

There are a couple of things that can be done to eradicate them. Spraying around the house with a pesticide such as outdoor Raid and spraying around the inside of windows with something like Home Control Ortho may help. Are indoor sprays harmful? There are fly strips to hang in the attic that are supposed to help. All these things work to some extent, but don't be surprised if they still cover your windows. I personally don't like any of these methods.

I heard of one creative way of disposing of a few. From a florist purchase a Venus flytrap, Dionaea muscipula. I suggest buying, rather than gathering your own in one of our bogs, because they have become an endangered species.

This small carnivorous plant has hinged trap-like leaves. Near the center of the leaves are sensitive hairs that respond to the slightest pressure which will trigger the leaf to fold in less than a second. The bristly edges interlock, trapping the insect. The leaf will remain closed until the plant's enzymes dissolve the prisoner.

You will probably have to feed the flies to the leaves, because of the sluggish nature of cluster flies, except when caught between a hot light bulb and a lamp shade. It might be an interesting study for your children this winter.

My father, had another solution. He kept a pet spider in our basement. He would catch the unwanted flies and give them to his friend whose web was over his workbench.

One solution that I like helps out our favorite bird, the chickadee. I open the window and brush those pesky flies out into the cold. The minute they hit the below-freezing weather they drop "like flies" where our bird friends use them to enrich their diet.

But the easiest solution is the hand-held vacuum. Still on sunny days, they keep appearing on our windows.

It was a common belief, mentioned by Aristotle and persisting into the 17th century, that insects were spontaneously generated.

With the evidence before my eyes, I'm inclined to agree with the spontaneous generation theory. I'm sorry Dr. Merritt.

Winter

The Beauty and Problems of Snow

The weathermen sent out their warnings; a winter storm watch, with from six to twelve inches of snow. The first major snow of the season and we were ready. The Old Sea Dog had shifted things around in the garage so that the snow blower was easily accessible. He had filled its tank with gas and tested its starting. The snow shovels were in place. I had found my deer skin choppers, and re-waterproofed my boots.

It came in the night, and by morning we had over ten inches of wet snow, and still it came. Our spruce and white pine branches were bent with the weight. Everything was gray and white and beautiful.

We put more seed in the feeders, even before I made the coffee and fortifying hot cereal.

As a kid I belonged to the "H.C.B. Club," the hot cereal breakfast club, a Ralston's promotion. Every time I had hot cereal for breakfast I would get a gold star on the free chart. Even today, years and years later, when I eat hot cereal I remember my old cereal bowl. It was probably another promotion from Ralston, as it had a checkerboard design on the rim. On the side there was a picture of a huge long-eared rabbit, holding a spoon as large as himself, with the motto, "Find the bottom." When I did, the message was, "Yum, yum, all gone." I was a reluctant eater then, and my folks tried anything.

But I digress.

After our hearty breakfast, we bundled up for the outdoor task. The Old Sea Dog got out his snowblower, while I started shoveling a path in front of the door. The machine sprang to life and he made one sweep the length of the drive, and THE WHEEL FELL OFF — so much for the best laid plans of men.

I kept on shoveling while he propped up the machine and finally got the wheel back on. But, it wasn't seated correctly and the wheel wouldn't turn.

I'm afraid I quoted my father, "It's the fleas that keep the dog alive," as he maneuvered the blower back into the garage and picked up the other shovel.

While doing the monotonous work, I thought about a passage that I had read the night before in Edwin Way Teale's book, *Wandering Through Winter*. The article was about the fifty year obsession of Wilson Alwyn Bentley of Jericho, Vermont, for snow and snowflakes. When he was eleven in 1876, his mother let him peer through a microscope at the fragile beauty of a snowflake.

He was hooked.

At twenty, his mother persuaded his father to buy Wilson a compound microscope and heavy studio camera. The cost was about $100.00. "As long as he lived, his father thought this was an unnecessary extravagance," but snowflakes became Wilson's life.

In an unheated shed, he recorded on glass plates the magnified images of snowflakes. He would stand in the open doorway and collect the flakes on a smooth board painted black. With a feather he would separate the individual flakes and examine them with a magnifying glass. When he found a perfect specimen he would photograph it through his microscope, magnifying the crystals from 64 to 3,600 times.

Bentley claimed that each flake was unique, and his snowflake portraits bear this out.

When Wilson Bentley died on December 23, 1931, his magnum opus, *Snow Crystals*, had finally been published, but only three weeks before. It contained 2,000 of his best pictures.

My encyclopedia contains six of these photos. Each six sided crystal is an intricate jewel.

When my middle son was in junior high, he had to do a science project. Somewhere we found an article telling us about a poly-based chemical that would "freeze" snowflakes. We were able to obtain the chemical from a chemist friend, and his science project began. In preparation for the snow, he gathered a black velvet cloth, the chemical, clean microscope slides, and a fine paint brush to moisten with the fluid in order to pick up the individual flakes to mount. Problem, we lived in New Jersey at the time, and there was NO SNOW. It was getting close to the science fair.

One morning I looked out and it was snowing. Poor John was in school. Would it be cheating if I collected the flakes?

I got his things together and headed outside. A few choice snowflakes landed on the velvet. Beautiful. I had just dampened the brush when John came running down the street. A kind and understanding teacher had allowed him to leave the classroom.

The project was a success. The O.S.D. loaned him the lense from an old 35 mm camera for a projector, and John's snowflakes were reflected onto white cardboard. We all got to see the beauty and individuality of a few snowflakes.

Memories. I kept on shoveling. How could something so small and beautiful weigh so much?

We can get Down Our Road with our 4x4 U.P. Cadillac (our pick-up truck) but it will be awhile before the snowplow reaches us. The repair man got up our hill and took the blower to his shop. The wheel weld had broken.

"I've never seen that before," he said.

Back in the warm house, I enjoyed the beauty of the giant cotton ball covered branches, speculated about how each snow crystal can be unique, watched the chickadees, and drank my hot coffee.

Christmas Trees
for the Galleria

Early Monday morning we bundled up in the layered look, long johns, wool socks, turtle neck shirts, sweaters, and boots. It added about 10 pounds, but we were ready for the snow covered woods.

We gathered at the home of our Fearless Leader, H.B. We were eight hardy souls, all armed with chain saws and hand saws. One small, but energetic woman even brought an ax.

Our leader had already attached a large flat-bed trailer to his truck. The rest of us piled into two other vehicles. The caravan to bring back the trees for the Iron County Museum's Christmas Tree Galleria was underway.

The rangers from the Ottawa National Forest had assigned us our location east of Golden Lake. We followed behind H.B. who led us down the narrow forest road. It had been plowed only once after the ten inch snow fall the Friday before, but only into a single lane. The sides of the road were untouched except for a few places where deer had crossed.

H.B. found our assigned location and stopped in the middle of the road. "I'm going to turn the trailer around before we start," he said.

There was an unplowed cross road ahead.

H.B. had been an instructor in the U.S. Army during World War II, and had taught men how to maneuver trailers. He was good. In spite of the fact that his truck did not have four wheel drive, he managed the turn around, but it took a lot of back and forth.

Our instructions had been, "Don't cut trees along the sides of the road." In this location, there weren't any trees along the side of the road. All the potential Christmas trees were beyond a snow covered clearing.

The men with the chain saws set out to find the thirty-five balsam or spruce that we needed. Of course, we wanted them well shaped and full. It was sometimes hard to tell as they were heavily covered with snow.

The men cut, and the women dragged the trees across the field. It was hard going. The snow was well over my Sorel boots, and unexpected hollows even came above our knees. The Old Sea Dog slipped and fell, but he managed to fling his chain saw into the snow ahead of him. The air was blue, but he and the saw were all right.

Our energetic ax wielder found a tree to her liking and with a few well placed strokes chopped it down.

Soon, the side of the road was filled with trees. "Thirty, thirty-one, we only need a couple more."

Then our deserted road, was deserted no longer.

A pick-up truck, hauling a trailer with an all terrain vehicle, wanted to get passed, but we were completely blocking the road.

An angry man got out of the truck. "You can't block a public road," he roared. "I have things to do. Move those trees or I'll run over them."

We smiled. "We're almost finished. The trees are for the museum's Christmas Tree Galleria. Just a few more."

I guess he decided it was useless to try to get us to move, so he changed tactics and began to help us load the trees on the flat-bed. He even produced an extra rope for tying down our load.

By this time, we were all friendly. The men found out that they knew his brother. "I'm not related to him, he's related to me. I'm older."

Someone had volunteered the information that H.B.'s truck didn't have four wheel drive.

"How are you going to get back up that big hill?" he wanted to know. "Logging trucks have trouble with that one. Why don't you go back over the bridge, and turn left. It will lead you to Forest Highway 16."

It was time for H.B.'s skill again. He backed his truck with its fully loaded trailer across the one lane bridge and 200 feet beyond. The road to the left was unplowed, but thoughts of the difficult hill sent our Fearless Leader onward. Our new friend was right behind him with no way to pass. We all were glad when he finally reached his turn. We had delayed him enough.

Back at the museum, we unloaded our trees. We had done very well.

One of our crew had made a huge pot of soup, which we put on to heat. A board member had made sloppy Joe's and lots of super sandwiches, and our ax chopper had made delicious pumpkin bread. We were starved and it hit the spot.

Last week the Cultural Center of the Iron County Museum glowed with the promise of Christmas.

All of the trees we brought from the Ottawa National Forest were set up. If some were a little sparse in places, that is the way they grew in the forest.

The community came forth with their unique themes. The school children made decorations. Iron County's own Santa was present.

The center piece of the exhibit was one of our best shaped and bushiest trees. It was decorated in silver with a thousand and one lights.

It was easy to see why one elderly gentleman told us, "The trees bring back such wonderful memories." He had tears in his eyes.

The Galleria is over, but if you live near a National Forest you can request a permit for personal tree-cutting from the District Office. For a fee you too can choose and cut your own Christmas tree. It's fun, and something to remember always.

Getting Ready for Christmas

Deck the halls with boughs of holly, Fa la la la la. The Welsh, from whom this song came, and the English, did just that. They decorated their homes with holly, ivy, and boughs. Holly was used because its prickly leaves resembled Christ's crown of thorns.

In the Upper Peninsula we have plenty of boughs, but our native holly, winterberry, Ilex verticillata, is not evergreen, and the leaves fall off from the three to twelve foot branching shrub after the first frost, leaving the small red berries to cling to the bare branches.

One day in late fall, I noticed a nice winterberry bush growing along the road, not far from town. When I stopped the car and put on my flashers, I could see the bright red berries only a few feet from the road. But, it was on the other side of a ditch full of cattails. I started to cross, but with the next step I would have been in water over my shoes. So near and yet so far.

I complained to the Old Sea Dog, and he, knowing my determination to get some berries, agreed to return with me. We put on boots and brought clippers. Nelson Coon's book, *Using Wayside Plants*, says, "The harvesting of the berried tops of these shrubs does no harm to the bush, and in fact, is apt to induce a greater growth the following year."

The O.S.D. was concerned that I would fall in the swamp, so he heroically waded over and cut me about seven branches, just enough to put between some balsam boughs for our Christmas table. I wanted to leave most of them for the ruffed grouse, and other winter birds who love them.

This week I cut snips from the tips of some of our many firs, and wired them to an old wreath that I made from woodbine. Woodbine, Virginia creeper, Parthenocissus quinquefolia, is a cousin of the grape. It can be a real pest as it has two ways of climbing. It has twining tendrils and modified roots equipped with adhesive pads that cling to walls and trees. It grows in rich woods throughout our area.

By the way, its purple fruit is an important wildlife food, but poisonous to humans.

I come from English stock, and my husband from German, so we have two traditions to follow. Our Christmas tree, left from the Galleria, will be up soon. We'll decorate with fifty one years of Christmas memories, plus a few balls that survived my parent's years and a few from his family. Our creche, which has been a major part of our celebration, got a new stable last year. I love unwrapping each piece, the Christ child, Mary, Joseph, the shepherds, the wisemen, and the animals. A celebration of the true spirit of Christmas. I see in my mind's eye, the small shining faces of my three boys as they set up the scene. So long ago.

None of our family can come the many miles, but we decorate for ourselves and celebrate with the birds and animals.

We feed the birds all year long. The cost of their seed is part of our entertainment budget. The O.S.D. spends time thinking up new ways to keep our feeders squirrel proof. He thinks he's got it now.

His latest feeder is a large coffee can with holes evenly spaced around the bottom. It rests on a metal circle 1/2 inch larger than the diameter. The original plastic cover is replaced and the center of the lid, can bottom and metal base is pierced with a 1/4 inch hole. An inverted funnel spreads the seeds to the outside. A threaded rod goes through it all and is fastened with a nut at the end. The whole thing is hung by an eye bolt to the underside of the roof overhang. The squirrels have no foothold. We get some good laughs at their attempts. The feeder is not pretty, but it works—so far.

But, we are not entirely heartless. We buy peanuts for the squirrels. These are not city animals, and at first they had no idea what we were giving them. The blue jays were the first to learn, and another entertaining drama enfolded. Who will get the peanuts first?

November 1992's *Wild Bird* magazine had an article on different feed for birds. They suggested black-oil sunflower seeds as the best single food you can offer. "These small, thin-shelled seeds are easy to open and are rich in fat and protein."

The striped sunflower seeds are larger and have thicker, harder shells that limit the birds that are able to open them.

The finches, and even our chickadees and nuthatches, enjoy the niger "thistle." According to the article it is not a thistle. It will not germinate because it has been sterilized before it enters the country.

My father made a wonderful suet feeder that has been in constant winter use for over thirty years. It is just two equal sized frames, covered inside with half inch steel mesh, hinged at the bottom and tied with a thin rope threaded through two eye rings at the top. It hangs from one of our birch trees, and is the favorite spot for our woodpeckers, chickadees and nuthatches.

We also feed our friend, the fox. Every evening, after the crows and ravens have gone to roost, the O.S.D. takes a few chicken skins or pieces of scrap meat and bones and leaves them under a tree behind the garage. We even buy chicken necks and gizzards for him or her. We know it is a fox, because of the single file tracks and the thank you scat.

We are rewarded with an occasional glimpse of "our" fox. Another reward is the fact that our trees have not been girdled by the mice or rabbits for several winters.

For Christmas, we'll give our friends a bigger portion and they will give us pleasure throughout the year.

New Year's Superstitions, Even Today

*T*he church sexton slowly tolled the muffled bell, but with midnight's last stroke he removed the padding to allow a loud clear ring. Thus the old man with the scythe, representing the death and sorrow of the past year was rung out with a funeral dirge and the new born year, depicted as a baby, was rung in with joy and hope.

The New Year has not always been celebrated on the first day of January. In ancient Babylon it was celebrated in what is now March and April. In Egypt the new year began with the flooding of the Nile. It wasn't until the Gregorian calendar in 1752 that the official New Year's Day began on January 1st.

But some people still celebrate the beginning of a new year at a different time. Rosh Hashanah, the Jewish New Year is a movable feast, celebrated in September or October. The four day Chinese New Year and the three day Vietnamese New Year festival, Tet, begin at the first new moon after the sun enters Aquarius, between January 21 and February 19th.

Almost all of these New Year celebrations are based on the hope for a better year to come.

The first two verses of Alfred Lord Tennyson's poem, *Ring Out, Wild Bells*, follows this theme.

"Ring out, wild bells, to the wild sky,
The flying cloud, the frosty light;
The year is dying in the night;
Ring out, wild bells, and let him die.

Ring out the old, ring in the new,
Ring happy bells, across the snow;
The year is going, let him go;
Ring out the false, ring in the true."

My beloved mother-in-law came to the United States as a young girl of sixteen from Germany. She was full of old world superstitions. When you forgot something and had to return to the house for it, it was bad luck if you failed to sit down first before leaving again. Visitors had to leave by the same door they came in. Spilled salt required taking a pinch with your right hand and throwing it over your left shoulder.

On her first visit after the new year, she would bring us three essential things, a piece of bread, a packet of salt, and a silver coin. We had to place them outside the window over night, and the next morning put them on the top shelf of the kitchen cupboard.

Bread the staff of life, symbolizes all food. Salt is an essential part of the diet and is the symbolic enemy of decay. Salt is also an element of the holy water used in exorcism. And it is good to have money, especially when you don't have much.

Her superstitions didn't hurt us, and who knows, they may have helped. At least we always had a quarter, even if it was in the top of the cupboard.

In Great Britain, it was customary that just before midnight a dark man, preferably a bachelor, would leave the house. After the last stroke of twelve, he would knock on the door, and when admitted would walk through the house, leaving token gifts of the needs of the household: coal, bread, and money. Then he would exit from another door. This was called "First Foot", or "Lucky Bird." It was an ill omen if there should be something unusual about his appearance.

He should not have crossed eyes, or eyebrows that met across the brow. He should not be a red-headed man or widower. Most important, the "First Foot" must not be a woman or a girl. This may go back to the time when there was an age old fear of letting a witch into the house.

Those people whose first name began with an H, a J, or an R were most welcomed. These were the first initials of Health, Joy, and Riches.

Another superstition is that nothing should leave the house before something is brought in. The old English rhyme for the new year is:

> *"Take out, then take in,*
> *Bad luck will begin;*
> *Take in, then take out,*
> *Good luck comes about."*

This belief may be at the root of the custom, on Rivington St. on New York City's lower east side when the Old Sea Dog was a boy, of shopkeepers almost giving away their merchandise to the first customer of the new year. Again the superstition of "as the New Year starts, so will it continue throughout the rest of the year."

A good friend told me about her visit to Greece on New Year's Eve. While the bells tolled in the coming year, each person tried to eat twelve grapes before the last stroke of the bell. A race for twelve months of good luck.

The O.S.D and I will make our New Year's resolutions (which we probably won't keep — how many years have I resolved to lose weight?), go to a New Year's Eve party where we will eat too much, have several cups of good cheer, dance the old year out, make a din to welcome the new year in, and wish our friends a *Very Happy New Year*. These are some of the customs of our times.

I hope the First Foot at your home will be a dark-haired man bringing gifts. We will be the first feet at our house after our New Year's party. Neither of us are dark-haired any more. I'll let the O.S.D. enter first. We are fortunate, his name starts with H for health, and mine with J for joy.

A Fur for Royalty

The Old Sea Dog and I were returning from town and driving the last lap of our trip down the county road. A slim white animal, low to the ground, streaked across the road in front of us. He was gone with a flash. The O.S.D. had seen him twice before and I had asked the question, "Does he have a black tip on his tail?" This one did.

"An ermine," I said.

Of course, the ermine is a weasel in his winter coat. It was difficult to determine his size in such a flash. When I got home I began searching my books for information about them.

The most obvious answer was the short-tail weasel whose Latin name is Mustela erminea. The books describe the males as 6 to 9 inches, with the female only 5 to 7 1/2 inches long, not counting the tail. Somehow, the one we had seen seemed larger. Reading further I found that the long-tail weasel, Mustela frenata, also changes his coat in the northern part of his range. He also has a black tip on his tail.

There is another weasel that inhabits our region. This is the least weasel, called by the *Peterson Guide to Mammals* the smallest living carnivore, weighing less than two ounces. He is only about 6 to 7 inches long, including his short tail. His body is no bigger around than a man's thumb. He too puts on a white coat in the winter, but he doesn't have a black tipped tail.

All these weasels have an anal scent gland, the odor of which is described as worse than the smell of a skunk.

Victor Cahalane, in *Mammals of North America*, says: "The weasel is the most bloodthirsty of all the mammals. Its favorite drink is warm blood sucked from the base of the skull or neck of its prey. It fills up on meat, bones, skins and feathers."

He goes on to say: "Apparently it kills for sheer lust of killing. Because it has sometimes slaughtered forty chickens in one night, people have believed that it lived only on blood. That was before naturalists began examining weasels' stomachs to find out what they really did eat."

G. W. Bradt, the author of *Michigan Wildlife Sketches*, says we should not condemn his slaughter too bitterly. "He is merely accumulating a surplus for a possible period of future scarcity, as economists describe similar actions among our own species.

When a weasel finds himself in the presence of a number of creatures which he considers his natural preys, as in a poultry yard, or a mouse nest, he cannot restrain his fierce desires, but kills them all. This wholesale destruction we view with horror in the poultry yard and with delight in the mouse nest. The weasel is perhaps the most efficient destroyer of small rodents known."

With his small slim shape he can enter the tunnels of mice, voles, snakes, and rabbits. He picks out the house of one of his victims for himself (he has no claws for digging). He may curl up on the fur of the mice that he had just destroyed. He has a certain amount of fastidiousness. He deposits his scat away from his sleeping area.

The changing color of his coat is not due to the presence of snow on the ground, but is triggered by the lessening daylight hours.

In Britain his beautiful winter coat has been used for the robes of royalty. When George VI was crowned king of England, his robe was said to have contained 50,000 ermine pelts.

In Britain, the Mustela erminea, in his summer coat is called a stoat. Perhaps the reduction of the species in the British Isles is due to the practice of hunting them for ceremonial robes, or due to the weasel's bad reputation. Farmers tend to shoot them on sight.

Our children all sing, "Pop goes the weasel," but originally it was a song for adults and had nothing to do with the animals.

> *"Up and down the City Road,*
> *In and out the Eagle,*
> *That's the way the money goes,*
> *Pop goes the weasel."*

The Eagle was a tavern and music hall in London. To "pop", meant to pawn. It is not too clear what the "weasel" was, but it may have been slang for a tailor's iron.

Last week the O.S.D. and I attended a party. The host is an outdoor's man and he showed me one of his treasures. It was a mounted ermine that he had trapped. The taxidermist had done a superb job.

I measured him with my eyes. He was smaller than the animal that had crossed our road. Ours had to be the long-tailed weasel.

I gently stroked his soft fur. How could anything so lovely have such a bad reputation? But like all critters he is a necessary part of our environment and the balance of nature. I love knowing that they are out in our woods.

Cutting the County's Trees

The County is having the hardwoods logged from their property at the end of our road. The trees to be cut had all been marked last winter, but the cutting crew didn't arrive until last month. Since then the woods have been filled with the sound of heavy machines and power saws.

Daily the log piles on both sides of our road grow larger. The once tall sugar maple and yellow and paper birch are now logs, cut into uniform 8 foot lengths, and graded by size and species. Sometimes we have to wait for the skidder to finish unloading. Twice we had to wait a half hour while the huge logging truck was loaded.

Worse yet, are the piles of slashings and the muddy tracks coming out of the woods. My Emotional Mind says that they are destroying our beautiful woods.

And then my Rational Mind takes over.

Rational Mind: You know that those trees they are taking have reached their prime. They have begun to decay, and will soon fall by themselves.

Emotional Mind: Yes, but do they have to leave the slashings. It will make it hard for us to enjoy the woods.

R.M.: How often do you walk in that part? It's been a couple of years. Walk in your own woods. Anyway, the slashings will help the deer browse.

The rest will decay in about three years. You know that it is part of the life cycle and will help mulch the forest floor..

E.M.: Three years! The county road is supposed to be a scenic drive.

R.M.: When spring comes, you'll never see the slashings. The loggers are removing the decaying canopy and that will allow the smaller trees to spread, and give them space to grow into more valuable trees. Remember, trees are a renewable resource. The sunshine coming to the forest floor might even bring out some flowers that haven't grown there for a long time.

E.M.: Those big maples were there long before I was born. I'll bet they produced lots of maple syrup. Those biggest ones were probably there for the Indians.

R.M.: Planning to go into the syrup business at your age? Don't make me laugh.

Also, you're a big reader, aren't you? What would you do if there was no more paper for those nice books and magazines you enjoy? The loggers will sell those hardwoods to Mead or Champion for the making of high quality paper.

And aren't you forgetting the economy? The County needs the money for services. The loggers need the work.

E.M.: O.K. you win. I know that you are right, but . . .

* * *

My husband and I have come to know the man that runs the skidder and admire the way he does his work. This particular crew are real pros.

When we've been inconvenienced for a short time (where are we going anyway — we are both retired) we have watched with awe as the enormous crane on the big logging truck picked up the logs and carefully placed them just so on the truck. Then with his bucket the operator tapped them into place so that they were even on both sides. That is skill.

At the November meeting of the Lee LeBlanc Chapter of the Iron County Audubon Society, the speaker was Don Schwandt, forest manager for Champion International's Lake State Region. During his talk he convinced us that the big paper companies have recognized that they MUST become stewards of the land.

Champion has been training their foresters to think of the total ecosystem. Some dead trees with woodpecker cavities are left standing for the animals and birds. Buffer strips are left along lakes and streams. They have instructed that no activity of any kind take place within 300 feet of an active eagle's nest from mid-February to September, the eagle's mating and nesting period.

Throughout the country, Champion has been setting aside "special places in the forest" to protect unique habitat for plants and animals. In the Upper Peninsula, near Wildcat Canyon Creek in Marquette County, they have set apart a large 30 acre stand of tall white pine covering a steep hillside within their 1,520 acre working forest. Many of these pines are at least 100 years old, and some measure 26 inches in diameter.

Fortunately they are not the only paper company that has decided to look at the total ecosystem. In 1990 Mead Publishing Paper Division hired wildlife consultants, White Water Associates of Amasa, to provide help in evaluating property that they own in Marquette County.

White Water's founders, Bette and Dean Premo, both have their doctorates from Michigan State University, Dean's in vertebrate zoology and ecology, Bette's in limnology and watershed land management. They, with their associates, recommended an area owned by Mead near Champion's Wildcat Canyon, and forest property owned by Longyear Realty for special consideration. This area contains habitat important to rare plants, birds, and animals.

These properties all lie in the Mulligan Creek canyon, one of the Upper Peninsula's most scenic river gorges.

A unique cooperative endeavor has developed with White Water acting as advisors. Buffer strips are being implemented along the rivers, and wetlands.

Rare plants and animal's habitats are being saved. The logging will continue, but with respect for the environment.

As more and more foresters are educated to look to the future, the forests will continue to provide wood for our needs, and a place for flora and fauna.

My Emotional Mind, and my Rational Mind like that.

The Deep Freeze

This deep freeze is getting monotonous. We've had six days of below zero weather. This morning it was minus 30 degrees on our thermometer. All the schools are closed. Today, at least, the sun is shining, but day before yesterday it snowed and was gloomy. Where did I get the idea that it couldn't snow when it was so cold?

"Silent, and soft, and slow/ Descends the snow." Longfellow.

The Christmas decorations were put away for another year, and the house seemed bare. On Sunday I dug out the dried bouquets of weeds and grasses with their shades of light and dark earth tones, with an occasional accent of dark red berries. I had hidden them away during the holidays. They looked great in October, but now they do nothing to brighten up the house.

I had also hidden away a branch of red-osier dogwood, Cornus stolonifera Michaux, that I had cut last fall. I had cut it simply because I love the red bark. I found an old carnival glass vase that had belonged to the family, and shoved the branch in. The size and balance was good, but it still was too drab. Then I thought, VALENTINE'S DAY.

I spent the rest of the morning cutting out red hearts from Christmas card envelopes. On them I pasted little colored pictures of birds and animals from cards and magazines. Of course, two of these are chickadees. I hung the hearts on the branches with red thread. It wouldn't win a contest, but it pleases me, and the Old Sea Dog said, "That's Nice." Praise enough for me.

There are lots of things I should do around the house. My closets are a wreck. For weeks I have been telling myself to dig out those still good clothes that no longer fit my expanded waistline and take them to the collection center. But I keep procrastinating. Not today, I say again.

There is birdseed on the living-room carpet waiting for me to clean it up.

There is a pile of Christmas cards waiting for me to check addresses, and letters to answer.

There are piles of newspaper clippings waiting to be filed where I'll never find them again.

There are recipes that should be weeded out. There are a few that should be tried. The O.S.D. complains that I don't make deserts any more. What I'm really doing is trying not to. Both of us need to watch the calories and the fat. Still, I keep clipping the BEST sounding ones. "Fold in one cup of whipping cream."

Instead I wandered aimlessly around the house. Read a paragraph from a book, put on an old record of the Mills Brothers and Tommy Dorsey, and dusted the top of the TV with my sleeve.

The chickadees kept at their task. They have a mission. I have never been able to count how many we have. A wildlife article says that they each need more than 250 sunflower seeds daily when the temperature drops below zero.

The O.S.D. was in town when the snow finally tapered off, so I bundled up in boots, scarf, wool hat, deerskin choppers, and warm jacket and forced myself to go out and shovel the three inches of snow in the drive. The wind whipped around the corner of the house. The little dynamos were chattering and even dee-dee-deeing from the pines. They kept me company and brought a smile back to my face.

Whenever I feel sorry for myself because I can't go out for a woods walk, I pull myself up short. I have a warm house, warm clothes and plenty of food and hot drinks.

It's then I think of the people who came before us: the Chippewa in their winter encampments, living in wigwams, and sometimes nearly starving to death when game was scarce; my Pilgrim ancestors, who were sick and hungry that first winter at Plymouth when of eighteen wives, only four survived; the early mid-western settlers in their uninsulated log cabins, with the wind blowing through the crevices; and Washington's 11,000 soldiers at Valley Forge, the winter of 1777-78. Many had no shoes or adequate clothing and the horses starved to death.

Back in our house, it was quiet, peaceful and warm. I made a cup of hot coffee, and pulled on my mukluk boots with their "furside inside and the skin side outside." My shivering stopped.

When the O.S.D. returned from town he went out to his Hobby House, our second garage. For several months he has been building two large tables for the Ives train set he had as a kid, and for the American Flyers that belonged to our boys. The tables are so large (one 12-1/2' x 4-1/2', the other 9' x 4') that he is putting them on rollers so that they can be pushed aside.

When he got the Ives, his father forgot that their area of New York City had direct current. The trains used A.C. It burned up the transformer and engine! They finally got them exchanged. Each car is about a foot long, and the coach car is even lighted.

Today we went to town for the mail and papers. I went along to get out of the house, but most important so that there would be someone in the car and the Boss could leave the car running.

With the sun shining, I'm not so antsy. The sun shows the dust and it will take more than my sleeve. I'd better get at it. The O.S.D. is headed back out to his Hobby House. He's like the chickadees, always busy.

Woodpeckers, Friends or Foes?

It was great to have the temperature above zero. Better than that, the sun was shining. It felt like spring. That's what a 40 degree warmup will do, even at 5 above.

I had gone to town almost everyday during our deep freeze, but not out walking. When you get older, the ice packed roads are viewed with apprehension. The mincing steps of the elderly have become mine. It's called fear of falling. But I had to get out.

We have a pronged dandelion digger with a long handle. It makes a good walking stick.

The snow along the road sparkled in the sun and was unbroken across the field except for an occasional stalk of yellowed grass and a few clumps of dried black-eyed susans. This area is so windswept, and the snow so deep that the deer and fox choose to follow another route through the trees.

The tiny spruce trees that we planted about seven years ago, stand like sentinels in the snow. In the summer they are barely visible above the tall grass.

From the woods I could hear the yank-yank of the nuthatch. When it was well below freezing they stopped coming to our feeder, but both the white and red breasted returned with the warmer weather and the sun.

Further down the road I could hear the steady rat-a-tat of a woodpecker. It was not loud enough to be our pileated. I haven't seen or heard "old hammerhead" lately, although he is probably deep in the woods.

I searched out our drummer. It was our friend the hairy woodpecker, Picoides villosus. We have a pair that come daily to our suet along with their smaller cousin, the downy woodpecker, Picoides pubescens.

They are easy to tell apart, even though their black and white plumage pattern is almost identical. The hairy woodpecker is about the size of a robin, the downy about the size of an English sparrow. The hairy's beak is as long as his head, while the downy's is shorter and stubbier. Both species have short thick feathers covering their nostrils to reduce the inhalation of wood dust. Downy also has a fuzz of feathers below his beak. It gives the appearance of an adolescent's mustache.

With both birds the male has a red patch on the back of his head. The hairy woodpecker is a bird of the deep woods, while the downy flocks with other small birds and visits urban feeders. Hairy and downy will tolerate each other, but not another pair of the same species in their territory.

By the sound of hairy's tattoo, he or she was not searching out insects, but was announcing his or her nesting area. They start attracting a mate in January, and continue through April. Both sexes drum.

We love to watch them on our onion bag suet feeders. Their four-toed feet, two toes to the front, and two toes to the back, help them cling upside down, parallel to the ground. Their rigid wedge-shaped tails fold skyward at almost a right angle to give them stability as they pound away.

You would think that they would become addled, or have a dreadful headache, but they are protected by a space between their hard skull and their brain, which is further protected by a tough membrane. Nature's way of adapting.

Their strong beaks are good for chiseling under loose bark for insects while their long barbed and sticky tongues snatch up their find. Amazingly, their tongues are so long that they coil back into the top of their skulls.

If a tree is attacked, it is because the insects are there. Woodpeckers locate the larvae of the wood boring beetles by their vibration or their sound.

We view hairy and downy as friendly insect destroyers, unless or until we are unlucky enough to have one decide that banging on our aluminum gutters is a good way to tell the world that this is his nesting territory. If that happens you may feel murderous when he awakens you at dawn. Try to remember that they are protected by law. Statues of owls may help, or you can thank the alarm-clock and get up earlier and get more done. Their noise will stop soon, if territory announcement is their game.

A different problem is with woodpeckers drilling holes in a house covered with plywood siding. Here the problem may be that you have insect larva or eggs in the crevices where the inner layers are bonded together. Insecticides might solve the problem, but might also harm the birds.

In the January/February 1992 issue of the *Jack-Pine Warbler*, a publication of the Michigan Audubon Society, a man who had this problem wrote about his solution. Since the woodpeckers only drill where the insects are, you should "follow from the line of woodpecker holes to an edge or groove and you'll probably find the small entry hole the insect used."

The writer, David B. Crockett, did just this and by plugging all these small holes he was able to solve his problem. He used a spackling compound, which is a water-based thick white paste that takes paint or opaque stains nicely. However, he cautions that if you plan to use a transparent wood preservative or semi-transparent stain, the spackling shines through. Try wood fiber putty instead.

It was wonderful to be outside again. I walked all the way to the mailboxes and back, rejuvenated by the clear air and the beauty around me. Winter isn't so bad when the sun shines and you know that spring is coming. The woodpecker's drumming told me that news.

Cricket's Song in Winter

I t was another 28 degrees below zero morning! When I pulled back the drapes in the bedroom the lower third of the panes were covered with Jack Frost's handicraft. Primeval frost ferns twisted this way and that, interwoven with hoary spider webs. It brought back memories of my childhood and houses with no thermo-panes. Those were intricate designs. The whole window would be frosted on the inside and I could scrape crude pictures of houses and trees into the ice with my finger nail.

Charles Godfrey Leland, in his poem "Frost Pictures" says, *"Rich lace curtains, which nothing cost."* The poorer we were, the more curtains we got.

As I get older, I find I have more time for poetry. The poets seem to bring back memories and call up emotions. But that's their job.

John Keats wrote a poem, "On the Grasshopper and the Cricket", which brought back memories of a time when our boys were small.

> *"On a lone winter evening, when the frost*
> *Has wrought a silence, from the stove there shrills*
> *The cricket's song, in warmth increasing ever,*
> *And seems to one in drowsiness half lost."*

Someone had given me a rectangular aquarium, about two feet long. I decided to make a herbarium so that I would have a little greenery for the winter.

We went to the woods and I gathered some small trailing greens, some moss and lichens, and a clump of bushy grass, plus a bag of rich wood loam. I tried to arrange it all artistically, watered it sparingly, and covered it with a sheet of glass. It brightened up a corner of our sun porch and flourished.

My parents came for Christmas. My father loved to sit on the porch to read his paper. One sunny afternoon, he said to me, "I heard a cricket." We both looked in all the corners, but found nothing. "You must be imagining it," I told him.

The next sunny day, we were both quietly reading, when the fiddling began. It seemed to come from my herbarium. Of course, when I approached it stopped, but I examined the plants. No cricket in sight, but some of the leaves had become lacy. Something had been eating them.

I decided to experiment. I got some lettuce and put it in the tank along with a tiny piece of apple. The next morning they were perforated. I searched through the greenery, but couldn't find our little friend.

He became a welcome part of our winter. Whenever it was still and warm, he would fiddle away. We enjoyed his company. I continued to supply him with store bought greens and tiny bits of fruit.

When spring came, the plants had become leggy, and I felt sorry for the cricket. I would let him loose to find his own kind.

I didn't have time to return to the woods, so I carried the tank out to my garden. I watched carefully, hoping to see our friend. Surprise! It was not one, but a family, three different sizes of black crickets. When gathering the soil, I had brought in eggs which hatched. New eggs were laid, and with no winter's cold, still another generation. There were so many, and they were so quick, I couldn't count them all.

Crickets were not the only unusual "pets" that we had in our house. Our three boys were always bringing home interesting wildlife. Several times it was polliwogs. In a small glass bowl with a little muck from the pond bottom and a moss covered rock, they were the centerpiece on our dining room table. Small plants of duckweed furnished their food. Their metamorphosis was a wonderful lesson in biology. We were able to watch the hind legs appear with five webbed toes; the right front leg; and finally the left front leg, the front ones with four toes. The tail got smaller and smaller and the shape of the mouth changed. One day we had a couple of tiny tiny frogs which crawled up on the rock.

Providing food at this point became a problem. I read that their food had to be alive and moving. Chopped beef on a tooth-pick didn't interest them. I gathered aphids from my roses. That didn't work either. Rather than have them die, we returned them to the pond.

One son brought home red efts from Boy Scout Camp. Red efts are the land-dwelling stage of the Eastern newt, Notophthalmus. I would not recommend trying to keep these escape artists. If they are not fed constantly, they can get through the smallest of cracks or screening. Ours disappeared and a year later when we moved the refrigerator for cleaning, there were the dried up bodies.

Our most successful critter was the large wood turtle that we found crossing the road. "Tornado" spent one winter with us. He had the run of the house, but seldom strayed far from beneath the couch. He scared more than one guest by coming out at the wrong time.

Several times a week I would give him a swim and feed him in the bath tub. He liked chopped meat, lettuce, and fruit. After he ate, he would obligingly defecate, and it was easy to clean up.

One day I returned to the tub, and was startled to find some of the turtle's insides spread out in the water. Tornado was a she, and this was her egg laying apparatus. She retracted the membrane, much to my relief.

When spring came, we returned her to the same road where we had found her. We had all become attached to her and hated to see her waddle off into the grass.

Memories. All dredged up from one poem, one cricket's song.

The Continuation
of the Species

One morning last week after a fresh snowfall, there were two parallel sets of fox tracks leading from behind the garage where we put meat scraps for "our" fox. A day later, our nightly offering had been ignored. For about a week, Foxy came only every other night. What was up?

The "what" is what has been going on since time immemorial. The dog fox had met the vixen and in March our acres would become the home of from three to nine young red fox.

Our love affair with the fox began one summer about five years ago with the appearance of a young inexperienced fox, full of curiosity. She had a beautiful red coat, a bushy white-tipped tail, and four black boots. She was an explorer. Everything was of interest including the interior of three garages on our road. She was not at all cautious. She would investigate everything, and would allow us to watch her. We got about six photos.

One of our neighbors tossed her a piece of chicken. She loved it, and came around for more.

It got so that if she were near, when the Old Sea Dog clapped his hands and called, "Here buddy," she would come for our scraps. We never tried to get her to eat out of our hand, but our neighbor, L.L. did. He says they had a tug-of-war over a turkey leg, which of course, he let her win. He named her Renée.

We had a large dinner party one night that summer. Some of the guests were outside, and Renée came to call. Everyone got a good look at her as she circled the house. She even sat for awhile near our back patio.

Her sex was confirmed shortly after that. I was sitting on my neighbor's stoop one warm evening. Renée trotted up and preceded to sit down in front of us. Josephine went in her house and got some chicken pieces, which she threw to Renée, one at a time. She ate the first piece, buried the second piece, and then came back, gave a big yawn and squatted, bitch like, and urinated. A biologist friend says that this was a sign that she was nervous.

The O.S.D. was taking L.L. for a ride through the field in his small Heald Hauler truck. Renée heard them, turned and ran after the two men. Of course, they didn't know that she had already bummed a handout, so they too threw her some tid-bits. Foxy, wouldn't you say?

As she grew older, we saw her less and less. Then she must have met Pierre. That next spring, we were able to watch a vixen with three pups. The mother fox had brought them to a clearing near our upper garage. While she lay and watched, the chubby little ones rolled around, chasing and nipping each other, just like domestic puppies. We like to think that the mother was Renée.

Late last spring, I was driving along the southern end of our lake, when I saw a fox along the road. The poor thing had only three good legs, the fourth was dangling uselessly above the knee. Was she the victim of a trap?

When the car approached, she hobbled off into the brush.

When I asked a friend of mine who lived near there if she had seen the injured fox, she was able to tell me that she lived in a field behind their house. They put food out for her regularly. The surprise was that this poor handicapped animal was able to raise six babies who tussled and played in view of my friend's window. It is fantastic what the mother instinct can do.

It isn't only the foxes that have started their annual search for the opposite sex. February and March are also the skunk's mating time.

Skunks are not true hibernators. Up here in the north they build underground burrows, often with two tunnels. Sometimes they den alone, but usually last year's young and the older females will crawl in together and sleep most of the winter away — but not the male. With warm days he's out and about, and by February he's actively searching for his lady love. He may travel four or five miles to find "her." When he does, she'll usually be ready and willing. In about eight weeks a litter of from three to eight little stinkers will be born.

Our red squirrels are also getting friskier. Yesterday I watched as a pair dashed up and down two of our spruce trees and finally sprinted across the snow. The squirrels have made a run-way between the trees and our rock wall along the side of the house above our patio. There, the first one scooted into a hole, popped out another hole, and ducked back in.

The chaser was not far behind. He too ducked into the tunnel, but came out a different hole. Underground, it must be honeycombed, because he appeared at still another opening, but not yet the right one. He seemed confused, popped in and out, and finally gave up in disgust. No sooner had he gone off, than the chased one, popped out, "Where did he go?" She — I'm sure it was a she — looked all around and as much as said, "He gave up too easily."

According to my books, the mating season for red squirrels is at its peak in early March, with the first babies appearing about thirty-six to forty days later.

Each spring is the start of a new life cycle. It is apparent here at Boulder Knob. Look around, you'll find it is apparent in your neck of the woods, too.

Spring

It's Great to be Back in God's Country

There is nothing like your own bed, and your own routine. After 4,574 miles through 17 different states, sleeping in twelve different beds, and eating too much food in too many restaurants, it's great to be back home!

Don't misunderstand, the Old Sea Dog and I loved seeing our children, our grandchildren, the very special great-grans, and our dear friends, but home is where the heart is even when there is snow on the ground in April.

It was 80 degrees in Beaufort, South Carolina, the day we left for Delaware on the last leg of our trip. That morning we had been awakened by the click click of a female cardinal outside our window. Her scarlet mate was serenading her from the highest pine, "what cheer, what cheer."

Later that morning a red-bellied woodpecker with his black and white ladder back and streak of vermilion from the top of his head to the nape of his neck visited our friend's feeder. He is about an inch larger than our hairy. He was followed by the brilliant yellow-green female painted bunting. I wanted to go out and search for her multi-colored mate, but when you are a guest you can't just leave the table.

The day before, our friends took us to Savannah to visit Fort Pulaski National Monument. The azaleas in the city were in full bloom, shades of pink, whites and reds. They were gorgeous — full blown spring in the southeast.

Our friends and family all know how much we enjoy the outdoors. Some of the highlights of our trip were:

- The discovery of the paw print of a large cat in the mud beside a stream on the 80 acre wild Florida hammock property of our daughter-in-law near Pensacola. Her acres are a jungle of magnolia, sweet smelling star anise, prickly cat brier, and vines of bright yellow jessamine blossoms. Pete and his wife have spent many weekends trying to clear out paths through the undergrowth to their spring fed stream. It was there that we found the clear footprints. They were about a half inch deep, four inches long, and clearly four toed. A puma, mountain lion, or as we call it, a cougar, had been drinking. I tried to take a picture of the print, but I had slow film.

- Seeing the gopher tortoise who makes a home only a few feet from our youngest son's driveway in Bradenton. For such a big fellow, (about twelve inches across) he certainly could scuttle backwards rapidly when I stepped on a twig. Jim's house is surrounded by oaks covered with Spanish moss. He has a stream behind his house and the property is covered with saw palmetto and unwanted poison ivy that he is trying to eradicate. He hears owls at night, has raccoons that invade his feeders, and has seen an otter in the stream.

- Seeing white ibis feeding on a suburban lawn, anhingas drying their wings, and cormorants with necks like snakes swimming in a park pond.

- Visiting Highlands Hammock State Park near Sebring and walking on cat walks through a cypress swamp. The way the cypress knees grow up to support the huge trees is amazing.

- Visiting the 1670 Charles Towne Landing in Charleston with our grand daughter and her two little ones. That was an adventure of fast food in the park, concession full of screaming children (not ours, of course), a tram ride, and a trip through the animal forest where they had only animals indigenous to South Carolina in their natural habitat. The puma was hiding, but we saw bear, elk, alligators, bison, otter, and raccoons. It was a lot of walking for these two old folk.

• Watching a lacrosse game at the University of Delaware's stadium. It was the first one we had seen since our middle son, John, played in the North/South game in 1970. John is the voice of the Blue Hens, announcing the scores and penalties from the press box. Unfortunately, Delaware lost to Navy 7 to 14, but there were good plays on both sides.

These are some of the memories we brought back with us.

Will we go again next year? Right now we say no. In fact the O.S.D. literally kissed the ground on our return. I hope the photo I took comes out so that I can hand it to him next year when he talks about the circle tour.

"Stay, stay at home, my heart, and rest." (Longfellow)

It's Spring;
the Eagles are Nesting

High, high in the clear, cloudless sky he soared. It was windy and he caught the thermals, using them to glide higher and higher, only to plunge in dives and swoops with the next gust. His wings barely moved except to turn back to keep above the lake.

In the bright sunlight he appeared ghostly white, but his shape and behavior betrayed him. Another gust and the eagle was gone from sight.

Sheer delight. It was spring, even if the temperature was still below freezing. This was not his hunting mode. Was he performing for his mate in the tall pine below?

I had seen the D.N.R. plane circle the eagle's nest, so I stopped at their office to inquire if the female was nesting. I was glad to hear that we would have eaglets in the aerie again this year.

We have a telescope that we set up on our balcony. Through it we can see into the nest across the lake, but the weather is still too cold and unsettled to put it out. Last year we had 18 inches of snow on the 15th and 16th of April and the ice didn't completely leave the lake until May 6th.

About ten years ago on a July evening we got a telephone call at dinner time. Would we be able to take the man who bands the eaglets across the lake to the eagles nest in our boat? We dropped everything for this experience.

The nest on our lake is 67 feet up in a tall white pine. The bander scaled with ease. The hard part was getting himself over the rim, an almost impossible feat. Instead he used an extension hook to pull the two nestlings close enough to determine their sex and slip the United States Fish and Wildlife Service band on their legs. Before he released them back into the nest, he held them up for us to see. They were enormous.

Edwin Way Teale, in *Wandering Through Winter*, says, "The contraction of bones and more strenuous exercise account for the later reduction in size and weight. But during their early months of flight, they may exceed their parents by as much as a pound in weight and a foot in wingspan."

Throughout the time that the bander was examining their babies, the parents flew around and around the nest squawking the whole time. In spite of their size, their talons and beaks, they didn't attack. Strange, when much smaller birds will inflict a great deal of damage when their chicks are in danger.

I was a spectator at another eagle drama that I'll never forget. Over our wood, an adult eagle was teaching its newly fledged baby to hunt. They were interrupted by an adult kingbird and one of her offspring. The kingbird also had a skill to teach. While the mother kingbird dove and pecked at the adult eagle, her young one practiced on the pitifully screaming eaglet, who quickly learned that life is a struggle.

In the first formal survey of nesting eagles in 1963, only 417 pair were found in the lower 48. This winter their dramatic recovery was seen in sites along the Mississippi where hundreds of these birds congregated to fish.

Science magazine for February 18, 1994, quotes wildlife ecologist Stanley Temple of the University of Wisconsin as saying, "The number of American bald eagles has surpassed original recovery goals due almost wholly to the ban on chlorinated hydrocarbon pesticides. The ban of the number one offender, DDT, took effect in 1972, eliminating a group of pesticides that thinned eggshells, causing the birds' reproductive rates to plummet . . . Now, the eagle recovery is winging along so well that the U.S. Fish and Wildlife Service is considering changing the birds' status from endangered to merely threatened. After going up to 791 nesting pairs in 1974, two years after the ban, the total crept to 1,757 in 1984 and reached 3,747 by 1992."

I am proud of our DNR for their part in the recovery of this magnificent bird. May the eagles soar over our lakes and forests forever.

These Strong, Wonderful Wild Leeks

The Old Sea Dog is hedging his bets that spring is finally here. On one hand the snow shovel still sits beside the back door; on the other hand, the lawn mower now has the place of honor in the garage with the snow-blower put away for at least a couple of months. Not that our weeds need mowing yet, but with the way the buds are popping, it won't be long.

Outside the breeze is warm, but the weatherman has predicted a cold rain tomorrow, with possible snow showers — such is late April in the North Country.

A stranger has joined a flock of juncos in their gray suits and white vests that are pecking around on the ground outside our door. Through my field glasses I can see his identifying mark, a dark spot on his breast. It is a song sparrow. He'll probably remain here when the juncos travel north to nest.

Across the lake, the hills have taken on a greenish glow. In the lake a flock of common mergansers are taking turns diving. It is hard to remember that the ice has only been gone from our lake since the 23rd of April.

Every day we see more of our summer residents. The tree swallows and phoebe have returned, just in time to help control our black fly population.

Those wonderful sandhill cranes are back. A pair of these long-legged critters were feeding in a swampy area beside the highway. The next day one flew over the house. These are the birds that a friend of mine's nine year old daughter and dinosaur enthusiast calls the pterodactyl birds. It's always a thrill to see them.

The O.S.D. and I are taking our daily walks again. No longer do I have to carry my ski pole to keep from slipping on the ice, nor do we have to dodge the oozing mud.

Each day brings another sign of spring. I keep watching for the first blood roots and Dutchman's britches.

Last week the lily like leaves of the wild leeks, Allium tricoccum, sprang up overnight. Their bright green patches carpet the dense damp woods. It's time for leek soup.

The white bulb lie deep in the ground. From experience, I find that a digging-fork is the best tool for removing the tangled roots. I take only a few from each clump. I don't need many for they are VERY STRONG.

Each spring in Richwood, West Virginia, they hold a festival to the wild leek or "ramp," as they call it. Some ramp fans drive from all over the country to attend the all-you-can-eat dinners featuring this potent member of the onion family. The plants are thoroughly washed, the roots are removed from the bulb, and the leeks are boiled, leaves and all, either whole or chopped. Other dishes served are macaroni and cheese with ramps, ramp pie and ramp salad. Some brave souls will eat them raw, but if you try them, be prepared to be ostracized. It's like any raw onion, if you eat them, try and convince your love to join you.

I make a northwoods soup that is easy once you have harvested and cleaned the young leeks. Saute a cup full of finely chopped leaves and bulbs in a little butter or margarine, add a can of beef or chicken bouillon and a can of water and simmer for about 20 minutes. A dollop of dry sherry makes it even better. A toast round with a sprinkle of Parmesan cheese adds a gourmet touch.

For your own ramp festival you could serve a dandelion salad. Gather several handfuls of young dandelion greens, especially those first pale yellow blanched leaves under rocks and fallen logs. Fry up a couple of pieces of bacon. Pour off all but a Tbsp. of the grease; saute some chopped ramps; add a tsp. of sugar and a

Tbsp. of vinegar; throw in the dandelions and stir quickly to just wilt; garnish with crumbled bacon. You might even add a chopped hard boiled egg.

My leek soup must have been just what the O.S.D. needed. Within the week he requested more, so off to our woods again. This time he carried the digging fork.

Our woods skirt the edge of our old Finnish farmer's potato field. Thousands and thousands of rocks surround that field in high thick walls. Each rock was hauled on horse-drawn stone boats. They are a testimony to that families' difficulties in eking out an existence on that glacial soil.

The farmer's old barn stands solidly. It held a treasure of well rotted cow manure which through the years we have donated to friends, who in turn have brought us home-grown potatoes, tomatoes, and other produce.

I'm not much of a gardener. When I tried, the critters took over. There is nothing more discouraging than having the peonies that you waited for five years to have bloom, chewed off and then spit out. The culprit was a beautiful large doe. So, I stick to wild flowers.

Just since our last trip to the woods, the spring beauties, Claytonia virginica, had burst forth. I admonished the O.S.D. to watch his step, but there were too many to avoid.

The spring beauties have lovely pink or white blossoms with dark pink veins in clusters on weak succulent stems. Years ago I read that they are a survival food. They come from a small corm that is said to taste like sweet chestnuts when boiled.

I'd hate to depend on them. While digging up the deeply buried leeks, we accidentally got a few of the corms. They are smaller than a tiny new pea. It would take six or eight for a teaspoonful. One book I consulted gives them the name, "Fairy Spuds." I wonder who ever thought to try them.

The O.S.D. likes to wander through our wood to see what trees have died or fallen. His macho sport is to push over the dead trees that are still standing. While he looked up for the dead or dying, I looked down for the living.

Clustered in a sheltered hollow, made by the roots of one of the larger trees, I discovered the finely cut, light green foliage of Dutchman's britches, Dicentra cucullaria. They belong to the same family as the garden bleeding heart. A further search yielded more clusters. These had just begun to bloom. The flowers are like upside-down, waxy white pantaloons with yellow waist bands, all hanging from the same pink stem. Could these small trousers belong to the fairies who eat those tiny spuds?

To get the sunshine needed for photosynthesis they complete their life cycle in the early spring before the trees overhead have leafed out. A month from now all signs of these charming plants will be gone.

Further on, I spotted something under the dried brown leaves. To my delight, on two decaying pieces of wood were six round, white fungus cups lined with brilliant red. They ranged in diameter from the size of a quarter to a fifty cent piece. Although, I had seen them pictured in mushroom books, I had never before encountered the scarlet cup, Sarcoscypha coccinea. The Great Lakes area and northeast to Maine, is their only habitat.

We were ready to return home with our bag of leeks when I found my favorite shrub in bloom. The minute yellow fringed tubes (usually three in a cluster) appear just before the leaves. I cut three small branches to gladden our breakfast table. Leatherwood, moosewood, or wicopy (Dirca palustris) is a shrub from two to six feet tall with pliable branches. It grows everywhere in the rich, moist woods of our area. The Indians and early settlers used strips of the bark for baskets and cordage.

We trudged back home, the O.S.D with the leeks and digging fork; I with my odds and ends of branches, fungus, and enough spring beauties for the small vase in my kitchen window.

As I was cleaning the leeks for the Boss's soup, I caught a flash of red at the window. THE MALE HUMMINGBIRDS WERE BACK! Lunch had to wait until I boiled up the sugar syrup for their feeders. I know my priorities.

Bringing Home the May

I t is the first of May! Time to go a-maying. From earliest times the beginning of spring, and the rebirth of Nature, has been celebrated with joy and superstition. The Romans celebrated from April 28th to May 3rd in honor of Flora, the goddess of flowers.

The Anglo-Saxons called this month thrimilce, because the cows could be milked three times a day. The present name probably comes from Maia, the goddess of growth and increase.

The young people in Britain would flock to the woods, bringing home garlands of early spring flowers to festoon the outside of their homes, and to the dismay of their elders, "indulge in wanton dalliances."

In England, the hawthorne tree would be in bloom and it became known as the mayflower. The queen of the May would be crowned with its blossoms and a maypole would be set up in the village green. Dancers carrying the bright streamers attached to the pole would skip around and around, weaving the ribbons into a colorful pattern. There would be singing and drinking of May wine — a dry wine flavored with the early blossoms of the herb woodruff. May Day was a joyous celebration in honor of fertility and good luck.

But probably because of the hawthorne's unpleasant odor, it came to be associated with death if brought into the house. "If into the house you bring the May, the head of the house will pass away." As late as 1985 in a book *Unlucky Plants*, published in Essex, M. Vickery says, "May must not be brought into the house . . . It is not lucky to even sit under a May hedge in flower, but quite safe otherwise."

When the Pilgrims came to this country, it was the arbutus that bloomed in the early spring in Massachusetts. They gave it the name mayflower.

I don't know if it was only a local custom, but when I was a girl we celebrated May Day by making small baskets. We would fill them with the earliest spring flowers, the small spring beauties, violets, hepaticas, adder's tongues (trout lilies), or Dutchman's britches. The beautiful bloodroot is often the earliest flower to bloom, but we found that it is too fragile for baskets or bouquets. The fun was delivering the May baskets to friends. We would hang our gift on their door knob, ring their bell and hide.

But in Michigan, all too often a cold late spring made it difficult to find anything more than a lonely violet or early dandelion.

Just thinking about this nice custom made me nostalgic. I decided that this year I would make a May basket for our helpful neighbor. From experience I've found that a cone shape will hold flowers best. I took a pastel envelope and sealed the flap. I cut about one third of it off diagonally and shaped it into a heart shaped cone. I glued on a handle, cut from the discarded part of the envelope and fastened it with a paper clip until it was dry.

It needed something more. I found a picture of a daffodil in a magazine, cut it out and pasted it on the front. I printed, "Happy May Day."

No name, of course, let our neighbor guess.

The problem up here in the North Country is what to put in the basket. My arbutus are in bud, but even if they bloom I will not pick them. They are protected, and I want ours to spread. Each spring I brush away the pine needles and leaves that make their winter cover, and I kneel in their small patch to get close enough to smell that unique sweet scent.

These mayflowers bring back memories of my father. Each year, when he returned from his spring trip to the Upper Peninsula, he would bring his young daughter a small box with one sprig of arbutus nestled in cotton.

This year I'll have to settle for small spikes of pussy willows for our neighbor's basket.

It's been a long winter, but as *The Song of Solomon* says:

"For low, the winter is past, the rain is over and gone;

The flowers appear on the earth; the time of the singing of birds is come, and the voice of the turtle (dove) *is heard in our land."*

I am always impatient for spring. I didn't have long to wait.

Within a week the woods erupted. Overnight the forest floor was carpeted with maple seedlings. The ferns uncurled before I had time to try fiddle-heads for dinner. They are supposed to taste like asparagus, just remove the fuzz and simmer until tender.

The trillium were in their glory, but without rain and cooler weather they were pink in a week.

All my favorites were out at once. The sides of the roads were white with the blossoming wild cherries and pale pink with the wild apple blossoms. The small shrubs or trees, called sugar plum locally, but Juneberry, shadblow, and serviceberry in other communities, started to loose their five long white petals almost before I got a chance to admire them. Botanists have difficulty sorting out the slight differences in the Amelanchier genera. Are the ones on our hill lowland, swamp, or round-leaved? I am no botanist, so I won't even attempt a guess. But I try to get to the ripe, purplish-black, juicy fruit before the birds. So much for a fruit called Juneberry that flowers in May, and ripens in July or August.

That week on one of our evening walks, the hermit thrush's clear flute-like notes filled the woods. There is no sound as beautiful. In the background the "teacher, teacher," of the ovenbird intermingled with the almost cat-like meow of the sapsucker.

Along our road were hundreds of yellow violets, golden adder's tongues, and yellow bellwort. Hidden in the grass were the white toothwort, wood anemone, and occasional creamy white clusters of the baneberries. Even the Jack-in-the-pulpit, that usually waits for June, had appeared.

When the Old Sea Dog and I were younger, we took long hikes through woods, bramble and marsh. We would take our canoe across the lake and find goldthread, bunchberry, and pitcher plants in the sphagnum bogs. Today we find it difficult to even get into the canoe, but I have these lovely plants firmly fixed in my mind's eye. I knew where they grew, and they are mine forever.

Earlier in this week our thermometer hit the high 80s. I enjoyed several blissful hours on our balcony. A stiff warm breeze from the lake kept the flag furling and unfurling. The sky was blue. The birds were singing. But with each gust, clouds of smoke from our white pines swept across the hill — pollen time.

I've never been bothered by these minute particles before, but this was the year. The pollen was everywhere. The shore of the lake was even covered with the life-giving yellow scum, which the O.S.D. labeled "yellow tide." That is life-giving for the pine, not for me. The streets in town were covered with pollen from the maple trees, and when I picked a sheath of grass, my fingers were yellow.

That night began my odyssey with allergies. I would doze off, only to be jerked awake by my coughing — then my nose would need blowing. The digital clock kept track of the hours and half hours. I finally got up and spent the rest of the night on the couch. There was no sense in both of us going without sleep.

In the grocery store I overheard a woman saying, "I think I'll give Mother Nature a calendar. She needs to know what season this is."

Is it summer? Only Mother Nature knows, and she always has lots of surprises for us, especially here in the U.P. But her surprise for me this year was a dirty trick. She dampened my enthusiasm for the out-of-doors for a few days.

What's next, Mother Nature?

A Fantastic Day
for Birds

Winter lingered so long in the lap of Spring, that it occasioned a great deal of talk."

Bill Nye, the nineteenth century American humorist, born Edgar Wilson Nye, must have been speaking about a spring such as ours has been this year. He was born in Maine, but lived most of his life in Wyoming. Plenty of changeable weather in both areas, but can it equal the U.P.'s?

May 15th, and it was wet and cold. The trillium in the woods had to be shivering. Our apple blossoms are about to bloom and a frost could be a disaster. Most of the day our thermometer said 32 degrees, and by evening it was registering 28!

But it was a wonderful day for birds! The female hummingbirds returned from their long flight from Central America, following the males by a week. These must have been our own, for they went right to the feeders. One female sucked long enough to make three large bubbles. She'll need all the energy she can get when the males start their courting.

While I was making the beds, I caught a flash of color in the budding lilac bush. It was a gorgeous chestnut sided warbler with his yellow cap. I had hardly pulled up the spread when the Old Sea Dog called for me to come and see the Swedish flag on the feeder.

"Swedish flag, what ever are you talking about?"

He was right. On our thistle feeder were two birds, a brilliant yellow goldfinch and a iridescent blue indigo bunting. We oohed and aahed over their beauty. Years ago I saw this same combination in our bird bath. It is a memory for the years.

All day the birds fed heavily. We had our usual purple finch, only now they are almost scarlet; our favorite polite chickadees; several redpolls (they had been missing this last week); and our two species of nuthatches.

Off and on all week I had been hearing the rose breasted grosbeak singing from the top of our tallest trees, but suddenly he appeared at the feeder. On his first attempt he did a lot of fluttering around before he found a perch where he could settle down to cracking sunflower seeds.

Then came the surprise. The O.S.D. was on the phone and couldn't come when I called. A male Baltimore oriole was feeding on our suet. Our neighbor had told us that one had been eating from the orange halves that he puts out, but we had never had one on our suet before. It stands to reason, as insects are a large part of their diet.

This fellow was stunning in his bright orange and black. When I looked him up in my bird book I was surprised to find that this is another bird that has been renamed since my childhood. Because of interbreeding with the Western Bullack's oriole, ornithologists decided in 1973 that they are one species and renamed them the Northern oriole.

If I ever see one with a white wing patch, I'll call it a Northern oriole, but until then I'll keep on calling the more brilliant oriole a Baltimore. Old habits die hard. What a shame to have them lose their historic name.

Orange and black were the personal colors of Sir George Calvert, the first Lord Baltimore, founder of the Catholic settlements in Maryland. The early settlers thought the bright colored birds resembled the old world orioles and chose to name them after their patron. They were wrong, our orioles are not of the same species but members of the Troupial family that includes blackbirds, cowbirds and grackles.

I want to keep this one close at hand. I hope he chooses a tree nearby as I love his song. The males find the tree, the females build the lovely hanging nests. Tomorrow I'll put out some strands of colored yarn for her with the hope that we'll be neighbors.

Beautiful birds on this cold day — but when will Old Man Winter leave Spring alone?

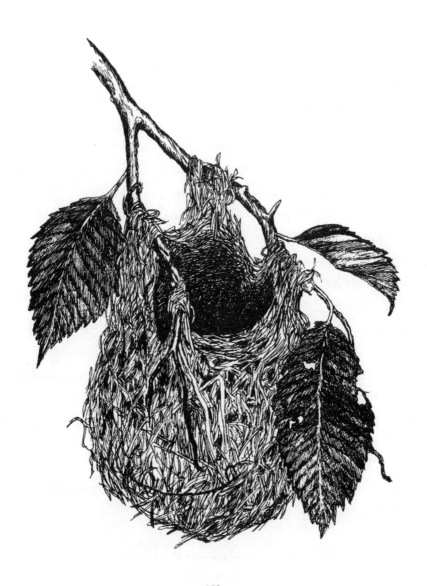

The On-Going Battle: Man vs. Critters

We live 85 feet above our beautiful lake. Getting down is easy, but the struggle up is not. My father found the answer and about 35 years ago when he retired, he installed a tram. It is a box-like platform that rides down the rails in three minutes and returns at the same pace. We depend on it to take us up and down to our dock.

Three weeks ago when the Old Sea Dog turned it on to return to the house, he saw a flash in the gear box, and it refused to go. After much huffing and puffing, and three trips up and down our ever steeper hill, he determined that the solenoid had burned out. He ordered a replacement. That took a week and a half to get. After he installed it, the lift still wouldn't function.

He called on our friend and neighbor L.L., a retired tool and die maker, and the two men, who can make anything go, set to work. It wasn't only the solenoid. There looking up at them from the inside of the motor were the two beady eyes of a very dead mouse. Even after the removal of all the mouse parts, the motor still wouldn't run. That unfortunate critter had chewed through one of the wires. The motor needed to be rewound.

The O.S.D. and L.L. are good, but this was a job for professionals. After two forty mile round trips to a motor repair place, much frustration, time and cost, we can go up and down to the lake again.

The O.S.D. thought this problem unique, but everyone he told his sad story told him one of equal or greater frustration — air conditioners, pumps, and refrigerators, all shut down by a little mouse seeking a warm home.

Critters and man seem to get into each others way.

One morning our favorite oak tree by the house showed fresh signs of the gnawing of a porcupine. The man of the house, bent on revenge, went looking for the culprit. Luck was not with the porkie, who was sleeping off his nice breakfast of tender bark behind our wood pile. The O.S.D. went for his weapon, a long handled shovel. Sneaking up behind the critter, he scooped him up and flung him, head over quills, about ten feet toward the field. The squawking, squealing porkie, didn't seem to be hurt, got up, only to be thrown again and again, until he was well out of our wooded area.

Last seen, he was waddling off toward our barn, probably mumbling to himself, "Why me?"

The exceptional engineers, and often winners of these man vs. animal contests are our red squirrels. The O.S.D. keeps trying his skill at keeping them off our feeders. All plastic feeders have failed, even ones advertised as squirrel proof. They chew through the plastic like it was peanut butter. One of our children gave us one of those sturdy metal feeders that adjusts the opening for the seeds to the weight of the birds. A blue jay's weight will shut it down. It hangs outside our living room window on the second floor of our split level.

One day one of those foxy red engineers figured out this squirrel proof feeder! While sitting to one side he would lift up the door with one paw and squeeze inside. The O.S.D. put his brains to work and jammed a narrow board in at the top, so that Reddy couldn't lift the door. Next it was the squirrel's turn. He pushed in the front see-through panel and slipped in, but this time he couldn't get out.

A good sailor always has a rope. The O.S.D. lowered the whole "cage" down to the patio. He put on heavy gloves and removed the top. The squirrel was trying to dig his way to the bottom through the seed. A friendly tap on his tail and he flew to the rock pile. We thought, "He'll not try that again." Ha! The next day, he or a close relative, repeated this folly. This time we left him thrashing around inside. We had an appointment in town. When we returned, this rascal had somehow gotten out. It has been two days, and he hasn't returned. We are crossing our fingers.

To placate the squirrels, we put seeds and nuts on the deck. I chalk this one up as a win for the critters.

If I insist on feeding the birds, I'll have to put up with the squirrels — and we do enjoy matching wits with those smarties.

Obsessed with Knowing the Flowers

When I was in grade school we had to memorize short poems. One of my favorites has always been this one by Alfred Tennyson.

"Flower in the crannied wall,
I pluck you out of the crannies,
I hold you here, root and all, in my hand,
Little flower — but if I could understand
What you are, root and all, and all in all,
I should know what God and man is."

It's an obsession with me. When I find a flower or plant I don't know, I can't rest until I find out its name and something about its history.

It has been hard, because I'm not a botanist and in the beginning the analytical keys to the families in botany books were a riddle to me. However, when I'm stumped I give it a try. I have to concentrate on what are sepals, calyx, and stipules. When I tried the key with agrimony it turned out to be a member of the Rosaceae family. "Calyx bearing a band of hooked bristles, Agrimonia gryposepala or parviflora, p.186."

My friend with the small yellow spiked flowers with the annoying burs that grow profusely along our road is a member of the rose family — hard to believe.

In the beginning it was easier to look through the photographs and drawings, to read and reread herbals, and ask knowledgeable people. Soon I was able to spot the similarities of families. For example, the mints, Labiatae, all have square stems and opposite leaves, and are usually aromatic when crushed. The Cruciferae, or mustard family, all have cross-shaped flowers and six stamen of unequal length.

Once I have identified a plant, it is mine forever.

I get a kick out of telling youngsters to pick that roundish leaf and rub the stem against their skin. They enjoy smearing it on their faces and pretending they are Indians in war paint. That is how my grandchildren remember the bloodroot. I caution that the root is poisonous, but was used for dying baskets, quills and fabric.

The early spring flowers are a joy. We have waited so long for their appearance. But the late spring flowers are more interesting to me, because they are not as well known.

This last week I found one of our most beautiful native orchids growing right in the middle of a path along the lake. The moccasin flower, Cypripedium acaule, was not yet in bloom, and is the last of what used to be dozens. Others use this path, so I made a barricade of rock around this precious protected plant hoping that it would be safe.

When I walked Down Our Road for my exercise, I spot many flowers that have become friends through the years. We have both the Solomon's seal, Polygonatum biflorum, and the false Solomon's seal, Smilacina racemosa. When they are not in bloom they are hard to tell apart, but right now the false Solomon's seal displays a lovely cream colored plume at the end of its almost horizontal stem which will develop into a cluster of bright red berries in late summer.

The true Solomon's seal has greenish white bell-shaped flowers hanging in clusters underneath an arching stem. This plant is a well-known herb and has been used since the 16th century to close wounds. John Gerard in his 1597 *Herball*, wrote, "The root taketh away in one night, or two at the most, any bruise, blacke or blew spots gotten by falls or women's wilfulnesse, in stumbling upon their hasty husbands' fists, or the like."

Another inconspicuous plants that I enjoy also grows along our country road. It is a member of the ginseng family and is prized for its aromatic roots. The wild sarsaparilla, Aralia nudicaulis, was used by Indians as emergency rations and by the settlers for root beer and medicinal tea. From a single stem it divides into three five-leafed branches. The flowers are three round white clusters on a branched single stem coming from the base of the plant. I love to nibble on the spicy stems.

Join me. There are many fine flower guides. Some are arranged by color, but most are arranged by families. At least one should be in the family of every nature lover. The common names sometimes vary, but look up the Latin name of these I've mentioned and when you find them along the road, you too will have them for your own.

The Miracle Cure that Grows in the Woods

The Great Depression made life harder for the Finnish potato farmer who owned our farm. In the late 1920s and early 30s, the family had to cope not only with poor rocky soil, insects, and drought, but the collapse of farm prices. A surprise crop gathered by one of the sons saved the day, and brought in more cash than the potatoes.

That crop was wild ginseng, Panax quinquefolius.

The name comes from the Chinese, JEN SHEN, which has been translated as "wonder of the world root," or "man-plant." It owes its last name to the shape of the mature roots, which have the appearance of a man with two legs and sometimes even arms. The Native Americans gave it the name GARAN-TOQUEN, which is said to mean much the same thing.

Ginseng was first advocated by the Chinese emperor, Shen-nung, five thousand years ago. Since that time claims have been made that ginseng will enlighten the mind, increase wisdom, lead to longevity, and rejuvenate sexual power. The desire for this wonderful plant led to a war between the Chinese and Tartars over planting grounds, and when found in the New World, led to trading wars and as much frenzy as the gold strike. By 1718, a boat-load of ginseng, shipped to Canton, brought $5.00 a pound, an unheard of price at that time. The high-point of exportation was in 1824 when 750,000 pounds left the

United States, but by then the plant had already been over-collected and protection laws were passed.

Steve Nelson, of the Michigan State Extension Office, informed me that ginseng is protected by CITES, the Convention on International Trade in Endangered Species. In order to sell the roots, proof must be forthcoming as to how they were acquired.

Protection laws have led to commercial growers. Eighty percent of exported ginseng comes from Marathon County, Wisconsin. It takes the patience of Job to be a grower of ginseng. The conditions must be just right. In its natural habitat it is usually found on a northern slope in a cool moist wood. It takes two years to send up its first three strawberry like leaves, and seven years before it is ready to harvest.

For years the Old Sea Dog and I searched our woods looking for any that the Pessonen boys had missed. About eight years ago we found one plant with its bright red berries. We marked the place well with a pile of stones and a stake nearby. Perhaps we marked it too well for the deer ate it off the next two years and it has disappeared.

Or perhaps it moved by itself. Chinese legend has it that ginseng glows in the dark and can move by night in the forest.

James Duke of the United States Department of Agriculture doubted such a claim, and decided to test it. He planted 1000 plants in an experimental garden. The next morning half of the roots had moved, or been moved out of their holes, but had not been eaten. He replanted them. Again half of the plants were disturbed during the night. Dr. Duke now professes some credence in "Chinese sayings that are hard to believe."

One Sunday, the O.S.D. and I visited a friend whose hobby for many years has been to grow ginseng in the woods behind his home. He has several raised platforms filled with rich soil and leaf mold. He starts with the seed which he plants for a year on a mesh screen before replanting them in their beds. Then he waits.

I was honored when he dug up a five year old plant and presented it to me. It was too young to have acquired the man-shaped form. It looked like a young parsnip root except for the growth rings where the neck would be.

Our friends suggested that I clean it well and air dry the root until it was brittle, then I would be able to either break off a piece to chew or grind it to a powder.

It is said to be bitter, but the Old Sea Dog and I could stand bitter for an enlightened mind, wisdom, and increased longevity. I think it is too late for the other benefits.

Summer
Again

Ben Franklin Wanted a Turkey

*T*he sun has started its trip south again. Summer is here and the days are getting shorter! The fourth of July is upon us, a time of Patriotism, Parades, and Picnics.

> *Hats off!*
> *Along the streets there comes*
> *A blare of bugles, a ruffle of drums,*
> *A flash of color beneath the sky;*
> *Hats off!*
> *The flag is passing by.* (Henry Holcomb Bennett)

Leading the parade will be the high-school youngsters in their smart uniforms — our country's future. They are followed by the veterans proudly carrying the stars and stripes. They know what it means to fight for liberty.

Stand at attention, our symbol, our flag is passing by.

Besides our flag, we have many other American symbols: Uncle Sam, the Statue of Liberty, the Liberty Bell, Ellis Island, the National Seal, and the American bald eagle, who was chosen by Congress in 1782 as the emblem of the United States.

Benjamin Franklin didn't agree with that decision. In a letter to Sarah Bache dated January 26, 1784, he wrote:

"I wish the Bald Eagle had not been chosen as the Representative of our Country; he is a Bird of bad moral Character; like those among Men who live by Sharping and Robbing, he is generally poor, and often very lousy.

The Turky is a much more respectable Bird, and withal a true original Native of America."

On the National Seal, the eagle is shown with its wings spread, holding an olive branch in one claw and arrows in the other. On military insignia and coins the eagle appears in numerous poses.

Just before the Civil War, a Wisconsin Indian named Blue Sky cut down a tall tree containing an eagle's nest. He raised the fallen eaglet, taming him by feeding him fish and meat by hand, and finally selling him for five bushels of corn to a white man.

Volunteers from the 8th Wisconsin Regiment acquired the eagle. They thought that it would be fine to have a live "bird of freedom" as a mascot. They named him Ole Abe, in honor of Lincoln.

Whenever they marched, Ole Abe would be carried on his shield-like perch beside the flag. It is said that whenever the soldiers marched with drums beating and flags waving, Ole Abe would fly from his perch and grab Old Glory in his beak, helping carry the banner down the street.

Abe went through four years of war, 36 battles and 50 skirmishes. During a battle he would fly above the troops screaming his war cry. Once a spent bullet hit his chest, and several times his tail feathers were shot off, but he was not killed nor were any of the standard-bearers who carried him. This was strange, for the Confederates, who dreaded what they called the "Yankee buzzard," had put a price on his head. General Sterling Price of the Confederate Army was reported as saying, "I would rather capture or kill that eagle than take a whole brigade."

After the war, Ole Abe toured the country with his handler, raising over $18,000 dollars for wounded veterans. He was returned to Wisconsin where he lived out his life in a large cage in the basement of the State House in Madison, dying of old age in 1881. His body was mounted with wings outspread, and was on exhibit until a fire destroyed the State House.

I get a thrill every time I see a soaring eagle. A symbol of strength and power. Can you visualize a turkey on our money, pinned on a uniform, or displayed on top a flag pole? And what about a turkey flying above the troops?

Sorry, Ben, the Congress of 1782 was right and you were wrong.

A Walk Between Showers

The Old Sea Dog was eating his lunch when he looked out the window. "Get my binoculars, quick, quick, I think I see the fox on the stone wall." When he raised his glasses I got an action report. "There are more than one. They must be the babies. I see two, no three. They are tumbling around and chasing each other." He grabbed his binocs and headed out the door.

I was busy making a cake. When the O.S.D. returned he reported that the little foxes were playing on the warm rocks. "I was able to get quite close. One has a black throat. They look real healthy. It must be all the chicken we're feeding them."

By this time my cake was in the oven, and it was my turn to try and sneak up on the family. I swung around through the pines and approached from the back. Two of the kits left when they saw me, but one very curious one, the one with the black throat, would start to leave, then turn back to look some more. He stood watching me for a good five minutes, ducked down, then his ears would pop up, then his ears and eyes. Finally we both got tired of standing still and he dropped down behind the rocks.

I saw a tawny spot on rocks further towards the woods. I looked through my field glasses. It was the mother stretched full length on a large flat rock. I guess she knew that I was no threat.

The air was so fresh after last night's thunder shower and this mornings cloudburst that I decided to go for a walk in the woods after the cake came out of the oven.

Our field was beautiful with large patches of orange hawkweed, clusters of ox-eye daisies, and in the distance a large clump of yellow hawkweed. As I walked through the grass it came alive in front of me. Hundreds of small orange butterflies were flitting from hawkweed to hawkweed. These were skippers, family Hesperiidae, of which there are over 300 species in North America. The most interesting thing to notice is the way they rest with their forewings upright at an angle to their flat hindwings. I watched them sipping nectar for awhile before continuing on past the barn.

I entered our woods by following a well-worn deer path. It helped to keep my feet dry. I almost fell into a large round woodchuck hole, but saw it in time.

The woods were cool, damp, and quiet. Where earlier this spring there had been huge areas of wild leek with their bright green leaves, now there were only stiff stems, some of them with their flower buds still encapsulated in a thin pointed membrane pouch. Others had broken through showing fifteen three-sided white buds. I ate one or two of the buds and decided that they would make a nice addition to a salad as they tasted mildly of onions. Here and there were last years brown umbels, still clasping the black BB sized seeds. Our woods will never be without leeks.

The jack-in-the-pulpit have finished blooming. The only flower I could find were a few late white violets.

The forest floor was covered with maple and birch seedlings, violet leaves, bloodroot leaves, blue cohosh (the berries are still green), and several varieties of fern. My favorite is the Northern maidenhair with its fan-shaped whorl of leaflets coming from a black wiry stalk.

An ovenbird broke the stillness with his "teacher, teacher," followed by three loud snorts of a doe telling her young one it was time to leave.

It was time for me to go too. When I left the shelter of the trees, I could see that I would have to hurry. Dark black clouds were rolling in rapidly from the southwest. We were in for more much needed rain.

Each day the O.S.D. and I count our blessings. We are the luckiest of people to live surrounded by nature's beauty.

Nests, Colonies, Hordes, and Schools

We called them Eenie, Meenie, Mienie, Moe. Several weeks ago they appeared one sunny day on our patio with their mother. I'm sure Mrs. Red Squirrel was glad to get them out of their home under the rocks. She looked exhausted. Her fur was patchy, looking like someone had pulled out the hairs across her shoulders. She spread herself out under the picnic table while the four little rascals raced, tussled, and chattered, and chattered some more. I was glad they weren't my children.

Each day they explored a little further and before long they were scampering through the branches. This last week we haven't seen much of the mother. Perhaps she has gone on a much needed vacation.

To encourage these scamps to leave our bird feeders alone, I put some stale bread, wheat germ and peanuts on the large flat boulder that gave our house its name, BOULDER KNOB. That night I glanced up from our supper and instead of squirrels, chipmunks or blue jays, there on top of the rock was one of our three little foxes. He was gulping everything down.

The Old Sea Dog and I got a very good look at him for he was oblivious of everything except the salty peanuts. I got my camera, but I doubt that the picture will come out, as the light was poor.

He or she came again the next evening, because of course we put out more peanuts. We knew it was the same kit because his two front legs were black.

Last night, his brother or sister arrived first. This kit's legs matched its tawny coat. Hardly had Light Legs started to eat when Dark Legs bounded out of the trees and jumped up on the rock. For a few seconds, they played King of the Mountain. Light Legs won the right to eat first, but jumped down and let Dark Legs lap up the remains.

Just before dark we saw them again trotting up the road together, followed through the trees by our third little fox, Dark Chest. These are the same three that I saw a couple of weeks ago sunning themselves on the rock pile with their mother.

Our neighbor asked the question, "If its a gaggle of geese, what are a group of foxes?" I had to admit that I didn't know, but promised to look it up.

The answer is "Skulk." One dictionary describes "skulk" as to lurk, or a company of stealthily moving creatures, thieves, or foxes. Our young ones have not yet learned to skulk, they are too curious.

In the meantime, we get to enjoy them.

This morning another group of young ones are playing on our deck and running in and out of a hollow log thàt we have kept in the shrubs for their enjoyment (and ours). Like all the young, they are curious and playful, popping in and out from the chimney-like log and scooting through the hole which the chipmunk parents must had dug out under the roses. They are so laughable with their cheeks filled with seed.

I found three lists of animal groups, but none of them state what a group of squirrels or chipmunks are called. How about a scold of squirrels, or a scamper of chipmunks?

However, we may have a bale of turtles if the painted turtle's eggs all hatch. Each year during the second or third week of June the female turtles climb our 85 foot hill. They find a spot where they can dig, then they wet the ground with fluid from their body to make the digging easier. Their leathery shelled eggs are deposited in the hole and covered, and that is the end of their motherhood for another year.

If no raccoons or skunks find the eggs, we'll soon have a bale.

I wish I could hear an exaltation of larks or a see a bouquet of pheasants in flight. Instead we have colonies of ants, flights of butterflies, nests of wasps, a charm of finches, hordes of gnats, and a murder of crows. In the lake we sometimes find a school of fish, or a bed of clams.

This year our bevy of grouse and husk of hares are missing. Could it be our skulk of foxes?

Gourmet Food
from the Woods

July is the month for the culinary delight, Cantharellus cibarius, or chanterelle mushroom. Last summer, I found only a few of these golden gems as it was too dry. But this year we've had plenty of needed rain.

I headed for my favorite collecting site, a nearby hemlock wood, where in good years they grow along the path.

The day was sunny and warm after the rain of the day before. Along the road the first few wild raspberries beckoned. They are winey, and sweeter than the domestic berries and my favorite fruit. Only three or four, but oh, so good!

The late summer plants were starting to bloom. The fragrant milkweed blossoms were covered with monarch butterflies sipping nectar. Years ago I read that milkweed buds are tasty when they are covered with boiling water several times then allowed to simmer until tender. The bitter milky sap is dissipated, leaving a bright green broccoli-like head. It tastes very good, and rather like asparagus. When I served it to the boys and the Old Sea Dog they turned up their noses and wouldn't even try it. "Another one of Mother's foolish experiments."

Nearby a small shrub is in bloom. Its tiny pink bell-shaped, five-lobed blossoms dangle in clusters from the ends of the stems and at the axis of the opposite paired leaves. Each tiny blossom is finely marked inside its cup with darker pink lines.

This is the spreading dogbane, Apocynum androsaemifolium. It is poisonous to livestock, but the milky latex-like sap, generally keeps the cattle away. The Indians used the long, strong fibers to make twine, netting, and even clothing. They prepared the fibers by soaking the shrub's red stems in water until the soft tissue rotted. The fibers were then beaten, separated, and cleaned.

On the path down to the lake I passed the old apple trees. The branches were chock-full of small green apples, but the beach plum at the water's edge had no developing fruit. Last year this tree was loaded.

A loon called. I looked up just in time to see him dive. When he reappeared, he was far from shore.

Although I am easily diverted, I hadn't forgotten my mission, chanterelle for dinner.

The rain had brought forth many varieties of fungus. I found two beautiful members of the Boletus family, but I'm not sure of them, so left them alone. Years ago my daughter-in-law's father was visiting, and he picked and cooked many of these. He claimed they were the same as he knew from Poland. I tried them then, but depended on his expertise. They were delicious, but there are several species of Boletus that are poisonous, and it's not worth the chance.

I did find some fascinating small fungus. One looked like a cluster of bright red berries, another like tiny flat-topped white wheels with ridges all around, still another had the consistency of wrinkled gummy bears.

But, no chanterelle.

Back home I got out my field guide. The bright red cluster are called red pimple fungus, Nectria cinnabarina; the flat-topped ones were indeed called little wheel mushrooms, Marasmius rotula; and the gummy ones, witches' butter, Tremella mesenterica. Mother Nature certainly produces some interesting fungus, and man, some imaginative names.

Two days later, I took our lift down the hill to our dock, and there at the bottom were my chanterelle! More than a quart of the beautiful lemony orange caps, enough for two meals for four. It pays to shop in your own back yard.

Caution: Be sure to identify chanterelle carefully, there is another mushroom the same color that is poisonous, the Jack-o-lantern. However, their growth habits are completely different.

Last night's menu, pork chops with chanterelle gravy over mashed potatoes, and milkweed buds. The Old Sea Dog and my grand-daughter turned down the buds, but my friend from Maine and I enjoyed them. Gourmet food from the wild.

All Those Stinky Skunk Tales

Just say the word "skunk", and everyone I know has a story. When they are dog owners they have a dog/skunk tale, but even if they are not, it seems that they can recount an encounter. They tell me those "funny now" stories, that weren't "funny then," like the one my friend tells of a skunk who entered their house through their cat's in-out door. But that is her story, and she is a writer, so I'll leave it to her to tell; she does it so well.

Of course, our family have our own stories.

Skunks can live anywhere. Once we had one that lived in our honeysuckle bushes, just a few feet from the house. He never bothered us, but occasionally his perfume would scent the night air when he was annoyed by a passing dog. Skunks are usually nocturnal so are seldom seen, but often smelled. That nasty odor can carry on the wind for a mile. They are omnivorous, eating fish, flesh, fruit, and fowl. In the summer the main part of their diet is insects: grasshoppers, beetles, crickets, grubs, and bees. Eating bees gets them in trouble with the apiarists, but skunks can't climb (it says in my books) so a fence should solve that. But you can't always fence your lawn, and the lusher it is, the better the grubs like it, and the more the skunks will dig.

Skunks also like fruit in season. I met one in our wild raspberry patch. Somehow, he seemed to have more priority than I did. They have also been known to eat mice, even rats or rabbits when they can catch them.

When we lived in an Eastern suburb, one warm summer night the Old Sea Dog went out to find our black and white cat, Sir Cedric, who hadn't returned home when he should have. Down the block he saw what he thought was the cat. "Here, Ceddie. Here, Ceddie," he called. Just then a car came around the corner, and the pussy let him have it. The O.S.D. undressed next to the washing machine that night.

One of our neighbors back East was a gardener. Squirrels were digging up and eating her bulbs, so one evening she set a Have a Heart trap. To her dismay, she caught a large skunk. Polly was resourceful, so she got a large plastic garbage bag, and pointing the tail away from her, she put the trap, skunk and all, into the bag. She decided that the most humane way to get rid of the animal was to asphyxiate him. She cautiously tied the bag to the exhaust pipe of her car and started it up. Later when she returned, it seemed to have done the job. She removed the trap and deposited the skunk, in the bag, into her garbage can. Imagine her horror, when later she heard a scratching in the can!

What next? She consulted with her neighbor across the street. They filled a laundry tub and drowned the poor critter. I don't think she used that trap again.

We came up north every summer. One Sunday my parents, our boys and I were on our way to church. Along our drive we saw a strange apparition staggering down the road. It was a large skunk with his head stuck in a brown glass bean jar. We all had on our Sunday clothes and couldn't think of anything to do to help him. I'm sure there was more than one prayer said for that skunk.

When we returned, the O.S.D. who had stayed home, had a tale to tell. He had been working in the yard when the skunk came up the hill. He went inside and got a B.B. gun and was able to shoot and break the glass, all except the rim around the skunks neck. The skunk stood still, but turned his neck for a better angle and let the boss get another shot. This time he shattered the glass ring. No raised tail, just a backward glance that the O.S.D. interpreted as a thank you. Our prayers had been answered.

When we recounted this story to our lake neighbor he told us that he had a similar incident. A skunk came up on the porch of their house with a tin can stuck on his head and walked over to Ed. His family scattered, but Ed reached down and carefully removed the can. No problem.

Alan and Mary Devoe tell practically the same story in their book *Our Animal Neighbors*. They also came across a skunk with his head trapped in a tin can. He was able to talk gently to the animal and was finally able to pry it loose. The grateful animal brushed his tail and body across Alan's legs the way a cat would do.

Skunks are basically timid. They will give you a warning first by stomping their feet. Back off. It is too late if they form the "U" shape with their head and tail facing you. They can spray or shoot a stream of oily yellow liquid up to fifteen feet from the two nozzles beneath their tails.

I have always heard that the best method for removing skunk scent is a bath of tomato juice, but in the October 1993 issue of *Chemical and Engineering News* they give a formula for removing the scent from pets. It was developed by Paul Krebaum, a chemist at Molex, Inc. I think it would be less messy than tomato juice. I haven't had to try it, but I always have the ingredients.

> 1 quart of 3% hydrogen peroxide
> 1/4 cup of baking soda
> 1 teaspoon of liquid soap

Follow with a tap-water rinse.

Clothes can be descented by washing in detergent with household ammonia or bleach.

The Old Sea Dog found a good use for skunk's scent which is sold in sporting goods stores for hunters and trappers to mask their own odor. Back East we had a stone bench not too far from our bedroom window. On hot summer nights a gang of kids would gather there and drink beer and play their boom boxes. The O.S.D. bought some skunk oil and with a few strategically placed drops we were not bothered anymore.

Everyone has a skunk story. You probably have one too. Just remember, when he stamps his feet, skidoo.

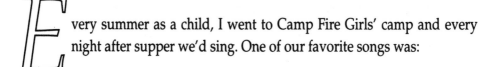

The Longlegged Arachnida That is Not a Spider

Every summer as a child, I went to Camp Fire Girls' camp and every night after supper we'd sing. One of our favorite songs was:

"They go wild, simply wild over me,
They go wild just as wild as they can be.
Every morning, noon and night,
Every minute how they bite,
The spiders, mosquitoes, and every fly in sight.
In the morning on my pillow case,
There's a daddy longlegs stares me in the face,
In my bathing suit and shoes,
Bugs assemble for a snooze,
They go wild, simply wild over me."

The Old Sea Dog can't believe how I can remember these crazy songs, when I can't remember things like where did I put an important letter only yesterday? I'm not alone in remembering the bygone days best. Two of my "old" girlfriends can sing this ditty too. One was a Girl Scout. It must have been a universal camp song.

It was probably at camp that I first noticed the daddy longlegs, grand-father greybeard, or as they are called in England, harvestmen. They would crawl into our tents, and as the song says, onto our beds where silly girls would scream, "A spider!"

I didn't know at nine that they are not spiders. They do have eight legs. Unlike spiders, daddy longlegs head and thorax are fused together into what invertebrate biologists call a cephalothorax. The separation from the abdomen is barely visible so that they appear to have no waist. Another difference is their pedipalps, an appendage that look like an additional short pair of legs above the jaws. These are used to hold their food in place while they eat.

They have been observed eating decaying plants, flies from spider's webs, and live insects. One investigator, Arlen Edgar, fed his captured longlegs on marshmallows, which they seemed to love.

Their closely set eyes rise like a conning tower from between their second set of legs, the longest and most important pair that they use for feeling and sensing. They also have a pair of scent glands that emit a fetid odor. One author compared it to the scent of a bedbug. Ugh.

Today I went out the back door searching for one or more. I wasn't disap-pointed. I caught one in a glass jar and brought it into the house where I could look at it through a magnifying glass. I was very careful not to damage its legs, as a slight pull will separate the leg from the body. This with their odor are sur-vival tactics. They can live without one of their second sensor legs, but not if both are lost.

I found several references to their cleanliness. They are especially careful to groom their legs by passing them one at a time through their mouth, holding them in place with their pedipalps.

Late summer in the north is the end of their life cycle. They die soon after they mate and the female deposits her eggs in soil, under a rock, or in a crevice. In the spring the young emerge looking like small editions of their elders. As they grow they molt, starting only a few hours after they hatch. Altogether they shed their skin seven times, each time leaving complete casts behind, even the outer skin of all eight slim legs.

We have two species living alongside our house. Mitopus morio, has a black stripe on the cephalothorax and is the most common. Our other is larger and is a lovely reddish brown and has darker legs. Species unknown (by me).

After I examined my captive under the glass, I took him back outside. Since then every time I go out our door I stop to watch these fascinating critters.

I was dismayed to find that our group have tried raiding a spider's domain. The webs by the corner of the house are full of long bodyless legs.

Should I spend the afternoon destroying webs? I want these Arachnida to survive. But then, they have lived for centuries and it will take more than a few spider cousins to make them extinct. We are sure to have more next spring, we always have.

The Fledglings and the Summer Storm

The day became increasingly humid, the first really hot summer day with hardly a breath of air stirring. With no warning there was a tremendous explosion. The house shook. Our visitor from Maine exclaimed, "What was that? Did something blow up?"

I reassured her. "We're about to get one of our famous summer thunder storms. I'll pull out the TV and my computer, and we can watch it come from the balcony."

The Old Sea Dog joined us, chased indoors from his outdoor project. He loves to watch the collision of the clouds over the lake, and as we watched he gave us a rundown of the wind directions. "See that fast moving dark cloud over there in the west. It's catching up with that slow moving formation from the north."

In the distance we could hear the low rumbles, soon followed by the zig-zag flashes of lightening and the louder booms.

All the birds in the neighborhood were in a feeding frenzy. Our feeders and suet were loaded with bird parents and their newly fledged young.

We had what appeared to be the offspring from two nests of rose-breasted grosbeaks, one nest of evening grosbeak, three baby red-breasted nuthatch, one mother hairy woodpecker with her big ungainly baby, and more finch than we could count, both male and female goldfinch, (adults only, too soon for their young) and numerous purple finch.

Before the rain came the mother hairy woodpecker took great hunks from the suet and carried them to her "baby" on the roof who was as big as herself. She would open her beak to the impatient young'n, who would stick his long beak into hers. Back and forth she went. He needed a lot to fill him up.

The red breasted nuthatch showed her family of three how to cling upside down on our suet bag. They were quick learners and were soon taking turns.

The purple finch seemed to have hundreds of mouths to feed. They went through a quart of black sunflower seeds in only a few hours. The parents would open the shells and take the inner seed to their fluttering babies in the nearby spruce.

The rose-breasted grosbeak young had trouble finding a perch not being used by the finches. I counted four young males with their red bandanna neck scarfs, and as many of their sisters or female cousins. We love the rose-breasted grosbeak and have never seen the young on our feeders before.

These birds have very commendable habits. The male helps build the loosely made nest and takes turns sitting on the green speckled eggs.

Surprisingly, to me, the female sings as well as the male. I couldn't believe my eyes and ears when I saw and heard the female singing her heart out from the top of our weather vane. I did some research and finally found an author who confirmed my observation. I also found out that they will sing at night, especially during a full moon. Our own nightingales.

Then the rain came — not a gentle one but a downpour, sending us inside.

Hardly had we shut the door when we heard that dreaded thump. A bird had hit the side of the house with such force that I knew it had been killed instantly. We looked out, but couldn't spot it.

When the downpour ended, my fears were realized. A male grosbeak baby, and a small yellow goldfinch were lying next to the house. No sense in burying them. The O.S.D. put on his work gloves and carried them to the foxes' feeding site. Every death benefits another species.

At such times, I feel guilty. Are we wrong to feed the birds for our pleasure, bringing them too close to the house? I take consolation in knowing that if it wasn't our house, it might be a hawk.

Mother Nature isn't always kind.

Another Year has Past

And so another year has past — another year with its infinite variety. I have learned much in the past twelve months by opening my eyes to our small domain and following where my curiosity took me.

Hamlin Garland, 1860-1940, was a Wisconsin born short story writer. In 1899 he wrote an article for *McClure's Magazine* entitled "Hitting the Trail." In this article he said: "I know the solemn call of herons and the mocking cry of the loon. I remember a hundred lovely lakes, and recall the fragrant breath of pine and fir and cedar and poplar trees. The trail has strung upon it, as upon a thread of silk, opalescent dawns and saffron sunsets. It has given me blessed release from care and worry and the troubled thinking of our modern day. It has been a return to the primitive and the peaceful. Whenever the pressure of our complex city life thins my blood and benumbs my brain, I seek relief in the trail; and when I hear the coyote wailing to the yellow dawn, my cares fall from me — I am happy."

Thank you for walking *Down Our Road* with the Old Sea Dog and me. We've enjoyed your company.

Bibliography

Bentley, Wilson and W. J. Humphreys. *Snow Crystals*. Mineola, New York: Dover Publications, Inc. Reprint of 1931 edition.

Bland, John Hardesty. *Forests of Lilliput*. New York: Prentice-Hall. 1971.

Bradt, G. W. *Michigan Wildlife Sketches*. Lansing, Michigan: Michigan Department of Conservation. 1951.

Burt, William Henry. *Peterson's A Field Guide to the Mammals*. Boston: Houghton Mifflin. 1961.

Cahalane, Victor H. *Mammals of North America*. New York: Macmillan Co. 1961.

Coon, Nelson. *Using Wayside Plants*. New York: Hearthside Press, Inc. 1960.

Culpeper, Nicolas. *Culpeper's Complete Herbal*. London, England: W. Foulshan, and Co. Ltd. n.d.

Emerson, Ralph Waldo. *The Best of Ralph Waldo Emerson*. Roslyn, New York: Walter J. Black. 1941.

Evans, Ivor H. *Brewer's Dictionary of Phrase and Fable*. 14th edition. New York: Harper & Row. 1989.

Fernald, Merritt L. & Alfred C. Kinsey. *Edible Wild Plants of Eastern North America*. New York: Harper & Row. 1958.

House, Homer D. *Wild Flowers*. New York: Macmillan Company. 1935.

Hubbell, Sue. *Broadsides from the Other Orders, A Book of Bugs*. New York: Random House. 1993.

Kowalchik, Claire, and William H. Hylton, editors. *Rodale's Illustrated Encyclopedia of Herbs*. Emmaus, Pennsylvania: Rodale Press. 1987.

Mowat, Farley. *Never Cry Wolf*. 1963. Many editions.

Muenscher, Walter Conrad. *Weeds*. New York: Macmillan Co. 1936.

Opie, Iona; and Moira Tatem, editors. *A Dictionary of Superstitions*. Oxford, England: Oxford University Press. 1989.

Peterson, Lee Allen. *A Field Guide to Edible Plants of Eastern & Central North America*. Boston: Houghton Mifflin. 1977.

Teale, Edwin Way. *Wandering Through Winter*. New York: Dodd. 1965.

Wernert, Susan J., editor. *Reader's Digest North American Wildlife*. Pleasantville, New York.: Reader's Digest Association. 1982.

Index